LIVING
THE LIFE OF A
Writer

6 PRACTICES
STUDENT WRITERS
HAVE, KNOW, AND DO

Jen Vincent

Routledge
Taylor & Francis Group

NEW YORK AND LONDON

A Stenhouse Book

Designed cover image: Getty Images

First published 2026
by Routledge
605 Third Avenue, New York, NY 10158

and by Routledge
4 Park Square, Milton Park, Abingdon, Oxon, OX14 4RN

Routledge is an imprint of the Taylor & Francis Group, an informa business

© 2026 Jen Vincent

ISBN: 9781032853109 (pbk)
ISBN: 9781003529514 (ebk)

DOI: 10.4324/9781003529514

Typeset in Garamond Premier Pro
by KnowledgeWorks Global Ltd.

For all the young writers who deserve to know that their writing matters—including my sons Jordan and Danny, my once and future students, and the writers who live on in you and me.
Don't never mind yourselves.

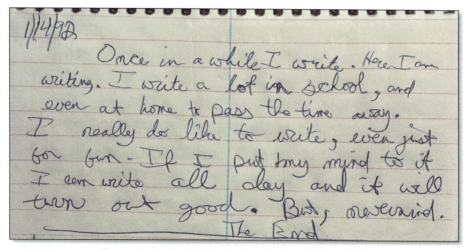

From the Author's Writer's Notebook at 11 Years Old

CONTENTS

A NOTE FROM THE AUTHOR

Dear Reader,

Or should I say:

Dear Writer,

You are reading this because you are a writer. Whether you fully embrace your identity as a writer or you write alongside your students, there is some piece of you that is here as a writer. This makes you a reader *and* a writer.

So, dear writer who is reading this, welcome. I'm so glad you are here. Connecting with other teachers is one of my very favorite things to do. I love teachers. I especially love teachers who are writers because writing is my passion.

My journey as a writer started in school. In fifth grade, Ms. Corn was my homeroom teacher, and I'm not sure what subjects she taught but one thing is crystal clear: my notebook. When I think about how long I have been a writer, I go back to that year and the journal entries I wrote back and forth with Ms. Corn. At the end of the year, she took me out to lunch because she used my writing for a project. I don't really know why, but looking back now, I imagine she was working on her Master's, and maybe writing back and forth with me was a sort of action research. Whatever it was, I distinctly remember our two-way communication in my notebook and that my writing mattered.

That same year, I had Mrs. McKinley as my reading teacher, and I remember working our way through *The Hobbit*, reading it aloud in class and discussing it. I loved the characters and the adventure they were on. I loved my notebook and that my teacher took the time to respond and dialogue with me through writing. While I was already a reader, this was the year I became a reader *and* a writer. This was when I started to understand what it really means to live the life of a writer.

Looking back now, I see how I have been on my own journey as a writer since then. Surely, living the life of a writer is not as perilous as Bilbo's epic quest, but there have been ups and downs along the way, and I've encountered countless opportunities to grow my confidence and persevere. I strive to share all of this with students and teachers I work with.

In this book, we will explore what it means to live the life of a writer and how you can go on this journey with your students. Together, we'll explore six practices that writers have, know, and do. While there are some things writers have in common, you and your students are on your own path of living the life of a writer, and you must each find your own way within these six tenets. I cannot predict all the twists and turns you will encounter on your expedition, and I'm not here to tell you exactly what this will look like in your classroom, but, like Gandalf the Wise, I am here to guide you, give you support as you find your way, and walk beside you and your students.

Welcome! And let's explore!

Jen

INTRODUCTION

The room was quiet except for the sound of pencils dancing along the page. It was our first free write of the year, and my eighth graders were practicing letting their ideas flow. I had introduced free writing, modeled on the board with my document camera, and now it was their turn to write. So far, so good.

I quietly moved around the room, scanning the notebook pages in front of my students as they wrote, when I noticed a hand waving me over.

I made my way to the far back corner and squatted down next to Marco.

He pointed to his left wrist and said, "Can I write about how I broke my wrist?"

I nodded, gave him a thumbs up, and let him return to his blank page.

As I walked away, I let his question settle in. I'm a huge believer in behavior as communication. Obviously, he asked me a question, but this question at this time gave me a lot to think about. It was early in the year, so I was new to knowing these students, and they were new to me. This was the first time they could write about whatever they wanted to write about, and what he most wanted to write about was his broken wrist. As an eighth grader, surely he's had opportunities to write in previous classes. Why did he feel that he needed permission to write about this specific topic? What misconceptions does he have about what is acceptable to write about? What has he read and how has that shaped his understanding of what is okay to write about versus not? Was this question a test? Did he want to know how I would respond compared to other teachers?

This moment stands out in my memory, and I share it here, at the beginning of this book on being a writer, for multiple reasons. To start, it happened at the beginning of the school year in 2019. This was my first year teaching middle school Language Arts as a classroom teacher. I started teaching in the fall of 2002 as a hearing itinerant teacher. For ten years, I worked in special education with students who were deaf and hard of hearing, traveling from school to school to mostly do 1:1 pullout work. After that, I shifted to working in instructional technology, and then as an instructional coach, before deciding I really wanted to be back teaching with students in a classroom. To be a veteran teacher who had spent seventeen years in education but a first-year classroom teacher was interesting. I had so much knowledge and yet so much to learn. I remember being proud and excited that we were free writing, and it was going well. I remember not knowing what Marco was going to ask me when he called me over. I remember feeling nervous but confident that this work mattered. Throughout this book, I'll be open and honest about my experiences as a teacher. I don't have it all figured out and that's okay. I still marvel at what my students and I do together and, truthfully, still face obstacles every day.

Teaching challenges me to know myself, to be clear on my values and beliefs, and to live them. Every. Single. Day. Marco's question caused me to reflect on what I believe about writing while also thinking about how to share this with students who come with their own lived experiences. I invite you into this reflection as well. We need to be clear on our values and beliefs so we can teach with integrity.

Ultimately, this story shows what it looks like to be a teacher who believes everyone matters and everyone has a story worth sharing. Our lived experiences matter. Our students' lived experiences matter. I will often tell my students that they might be young, but they still have experiences that have shaped them and those experiences matter. Yes, I am a teacher and I have specific skills I need to teach them, but I know my work won't get far if it doesn't convey that whatever they want to write about is worth writing about. When Marco asked me about writing about his wrist, I immediately gave him the okay. This is a small moment, but it stands out because it's a monumental way to honor students and the writing that's most important to them while helping them believe in themselves as writers. That is an empowering gift to give our students.

This book is meant to be a guidebook for teachers creating a writer's workshop experience where student writers can explore what it means to truly be a writer. To get there, we need to spend time reflecting. Reflection allows us to be honest with ourselves and to plan forward based on what we know. Throughout this book I will offer you *A Moment to Reflect* to support your reflective practice. When you see this text feature, I invite you to pause and take the time to answer the questions but also to carry them with you. Let them linger in your brain a bit. Let them hang around as you go about your days. Allow yourself time to contemplate how the ideas I share here connect with your lived experiences, past and present.

A Moment To Reflect

- What has shaped you as a writer?
- What was writing instruction like when you were in school?
- What do you believe about writing?
- What do you believe about being a writer?
- What do you believe about writing instruction?

BACK TO THE BEGINNING

I was lucky enough to experience writer's workshop as a middle school and high school student and then to teach using a writer's workshop model.

Essentially, writer's workshop is a student-centered way to teach writing. In this model, we focus on the writer as a way to teach students writing skills. Teaching starts with a mini lesson where the teacher offers something for students to consider in their writing, this can include looking at a piece of writing—maybe the teachers' writing, student writing, shared writing, or published writing. From there, students are given time to work independently while the teacher circulates and confers with writers: asking questions, listening, offering ideas, guiding writers to choose their next steps. At the end of the session, writers are invited back to share their writing.

To facilitate a writer's workshop means the teacher leading the workshop needs to be clear on what it means to be a writer. And that's where this book comes in. Together, we'll explore what it means to live the life of a writer, both for yourself and for your students. Whether you are new to writer's workshop or here to reclaim what writer's workshop was initially meant to be, I will help you find clarity about what it means to be a writer and give you ideas for making this practice clear to your learners.

We begin, then, with an essential question: "What does it mean to be a writer?" I absolutely love this question because it's simple and at the same time possibly one of the most complex questions ever. This has helped me interrogate my own thinking about writing instruction.

Donalyn Miller's book *The Book Whisperer* (Miller 2009) changed my life as a teacher because it helped me zero in on what real readers do. Ironically, in 2011, it was Donalyn who actually encouraged me to start writing for myself. Donalyn and some other teachers on Twitter decided to try NaNoWriMo, National Novel Writing Month. I joined in and started writing a young adult novel in November of 2011. I didn't "win"—write 50,000 words in one month—but I did continue to write and I finished my first draft in August of 2012 thanks to authors Kate Messner, Gae Polisner, and Jo Knowles. After connecting on social media and seeing an opportunity to support teacher writers, we started a virtual summer writing camp for teachers called Teachers Write. Suddenly, I found myself writing alongside these great authors, learning from them and getting feedback. Donalyn's work reminded me to bring what real readers do to students. For over a decade now, I've been on a quest to understand what real writers do and how to bring that to students. I've read many writing craft books and have attended author signings, workshops, and webinars. I listen to podcasts and audiobooks and read all sorts of different formats. I've read professional texts by Don Graves, Ralph Fletcher, Ruth Ayres, and Katie Wood Ray but also books about writing from authors like Anne Lamott, Stephen King, and Natalie Goldberg. I've soaked it all in. To say I became a student of writing is an understatement.

Soaking up ideas, reading, listening, and watching helped me come to some important instructional conclusions for myself, but I soon figured out that doing the actual work of writing myself was most impactful. With that, I've tried on lots of different ideas and strategies to see what works best for me as a writer. Since NaNoWriMo, I've been applying these ideas I've learned; from writing in my laundry room like Stephen King to writing morning pages everyday like Julia Cameron, from flying by the seat of my pants as I wrote my first novel to plotting out beats of a story outlined in *Save the Cat*.

All of this has helped me deeply understand what Natalie Goldberg meant in her book *Writing Down the Bones* when she wrote, "We learn writing by doing it. That simple" (Goldberg 2010, 37). Students need to be continually engaged in the writing process. This is what writers do. They write and, as they make their way through all its starts and stops, frustrations and celebrations, they begin to develop and improve their writing. Being a teacher who writes has made a huge difference in how I approach student writers and writing instruction because I'm in it with them.

After all of this, I've learned two very important things. One, at the heart of writing is a writer, and two, there's no one right way to be a writer.

In the work I do as a teacher and a writing coach, first and foremost, I center the writer. By centering the writer, we center what it means to live the life of a writer. Every writer has choices to make. There are universal things to consider in every part of the process but ultimately, the writer has to know themself in order to make decisions that serve not only their writing but them as a unique and complex human being. This is what writer's workshop is meant to do.

As a teacher guiding this work, this doesn't mean you have to write a novel or start a blog. But it does mean you need to reflect upon your writing life, recognize that you are a writer, and take steps toward writing more with students. Ultimately, it means *you* matter. Your beliefs about writing, your attitude, your mindset, your willingness to be a vulnerable member of your writing community with students does matter. Keep all of this in mind as we continue to explore the question, "What does it mean to be a writer?"

While this is not a simple question to answer, we can lean into it by looking at what most effective writers have, know, and do. In this book, we'll explore six specific practices writers engage in that I've noticed in my own writing life, in my work with student writers, and in my interactions with professional writers. Each chapter of this book will showcase one of these practices.

Writers Have a Way to Collect: This chapter welcomes you to living the life of a writer, beginning with collecting ideas. I share different opportunities for collecting, including a look at physical versus digital options and invite you to think about what collecting looks like for you and your student writers.

Writers Have a Writer's Mindset: Having a way to collect ideas leads directly into the mindset of collecting. Writers observe and notice; we pay attention to the world around us. In this chapter, I share ways to put our writer's eye to use as we collect ideas. I also come back to the ways mindset plays into what it means to be a writer and how it shapes our writing identity. I offer ideas for exploring what it means to embody a writer's mindset.

Writers Know that Writing is a Process: Now that writers have a way to collect and are paying attention and gathering ideas thanks to their writer's mindset, we will shift to looking at writing as a process. We review the typical stages of the writing process traditionally shared in school, and then look at ways we can expand beyond that to enhance our work. While we can trust that writing is a process, we can evolve beyond the basics to understand that things can (and will!) look different from writer to writer as well as from project to project.

Writers Know Strategies to Help Them Write: Navigating our writing process means knowing that there are resources available to help us along the way. In this chapter, I review strategies we have already explored, offer examples of some new writing strategies, as well as ways to find strategies as needed.

Writers Explore: Living the life of a writer means exploring what one needs along the journey. In this chapter, we will revisit the writer's mindset and acknowledge that writers are always exploring—whether it's ideas or their process or strategies. Writers explore especially when they feel unsure, stuck, or blocked. I offer ideas for how to shift into curiosity and to make space for exploration in living the life of a writer.

Writers Celebrate: Finally, it's time to look at celebration! Although celebration often comes at the end of a writer's process when it's time to publish, I assert that writers should celebrate often and throughout their writing life. There is a misconception that writers are tortured souls or that writing itself has to be a miserable experience. It's common to think of creatives as "starving artists." Writer Red Smith is famous for saying that writing isn't a chore, "You simply sit down at a typewriter, open your veins, and bleed" (Quote Research 2024). I strongly disagree with this. Writing can and should be joyful. That doesn't mean that it won't require hard work and focus but there is plenty of joy to be found in the life of a writer. In this chapter, I offer opportunities for when and how to celebrate and invite you to explore what celebration can look like for you and your student writers.

Overall, this book is for any educator who wants a more authentic writing experience for their students, who values student voice and choice, and who wants to take ownership of guiding their students through writing from an inquiry-based perspective. Teaching today is racked with overwhelm, lack of autonomy, and fatigue. We are doing our best to figure out how to encourage student writers. There is a tendency to prescribe graphic organizers or worksheets from Teachers Pay Teachers instead of creating space for student writers to explore what it means to be a writer. This is a guidebook for those who worry we have lost our way from the original intent of the writer's workshop and who crave flexibility and intentionality when it comes to writing instruction. This is your invitation to explore—for yourself and with your students—what it means to live the life of a writer.

Living the Practice: Activating Inquiry

Write the question, "What does it mean to be a writer?" on the board, your large format display, or on an anchor chart so all your students can see it. Ask them to write the question in their notebooks. Give them time to think about how they would answer this question. You have options here: they can turn and talk to an elbow partner, they can write their answers independently in their notebooks, or vice versa. After you have given students time to chat and/or write, invite them to share with the group. Record their ideas and invite them to add any new understandings to their notebooks. Ask questions to clarify their thinking and push their thinking where you can. While leading this discussion with a group of eighth graders, two students were chatting and I asked, "Does this count as living the life of a writer?" One responded, "Well, it's *part* of it." They argued that you can't just talk out ideas, eventually you have to write them down.

The goal of this conversation is to invite students to think about the question, not to come to any absolutes. They might have ideas you didn't think of when you made your list. They might have very different ideas from what you want them to have. That's okay! You might recognize some misconceptions you can address (in due time) or some areas where you can expand on their thinking. For example, a seventh-grade student suggested, "Writers publish their writing." I responded by asking whether you have to be published to be a writer, and several students in class said no. You and your students might move further into understanding some previous experiences with writing. If you'd like, invite them to tell you more about what writing has been like in school for them and ask them if they write outside of school and how that writing is similar or different. Their answers will no doubt give you information to guide you as you help them explore what it means to live the life of a writer.

> ## What does it mean to be a writer?
>
> * Use words to make a story
> * Use creativity
> * be observant
> * express yourself
> * Use your imagination
> * Come up with ideas
> * have multiple ideas
> * use past ideas
> * do research and include facts
> * think about the reader
> * WRITE! • stories • texts • emails • scripts
> * make choices that work for them
> * make rough drafts
> * make writing better
> * put ideas together
> * write for yourself or others

What does it mean to be a writer?

- Writes about what is in their mind or made up situations
- Throw ideas out into the world
- Make stories
- Publish them
- Having someone read your story, they can summarize
- Writers read - their own work and others' work
- Need to care for writing - to make it the best it can be, work hard at it
- Writers are creative
- Writers research
- Shares ideas or opinions
- Writers share ideas to get feedback
- Brainstorming is part of being a writer

What does it mean to be a writer?

- To turn an idea into something on a page
- Putting thought into your writing
- They write
- Diving deep into things you care about
- Writing to make others connect with something you care about
- Using your creative imagination and expertise to share information with words or text
- Writes stories, books, poems, comics
- Write and share ideas
- Put thought into their writing
- A writer makes people see things in a different way in their mind

---

We will come back to this question of what it means to live the life of a writer again and again, for ourselves and with our student writers. You can keep this anchor chart handy and refer back to it as you dive deeper into exploring all the various ways you and your student writers can live the life of a writer.

And now, it's time to celebrate! As I shared earlier, living the life of a writer can and should be joyful…but that doesn't mean that we won't experience other emotions as well. In my experience working with teachers, there are a range of emotions that you might be feeling right now. Depending on your experience with teaching writing, you might feel wary, unsure, nervous, scared, annoyed, overwhelmed, frustrated, irritated, mad, hopeful, cautious, optimistic, excited, eager, relieved, thankful, or any combination of these feelings.

A Moment To Reflect

Take a few minutes to check in with yourself and acknowledge the emotions that are present right now. Make a list of what emotions you are feeling. If you have a sense of why these emotions are present, write about that too. Remember that your students will likely feel a range of emotions when it comes to writing, just like you.

FEELING OUR WAY FORWARD

I'd like to celebrate by sharing and honoring what I'm feeling as we set off on this adventure.

First, I'm feeling grateful that you are here to explore what it means to live the life of a writer with me and to share this way of approaching writing with your students. Approaching writing instruction with an open mind and with a sense of curiosity to explore is very different from assigning a paper or teaching a five-paragraph essay. Your willingness to embrace exploration is admirable.

Next, I'm feeling excited to be your guide as we explore the six practices writers have, know, and do because I know firsthand the power of writer's workshop thanks to my own middle school and high school teachers. Writer's workshop gave me confidence in myself, my abilities, but also my stories. I'm thrilled to share this with you and, in turn, your students.

And, finally, I'm filled with a sense of solidarity and hope. We truly are in this together. When I think of teachers like you who help students tell their stories, share what they know, and express their opinions, I feel empowered. I hope you also feel empowered to do this work. Remember that I'm here to guide you on this journey.

Let's start by looking at how writers have a way to collect. Onward!

CHAPTER 1

Writers Have a Way to Collect

I was a hearing itinerant teacher working 1:1 with students or in small groups when I designed my first writer's notebook. It was 2009 and I had read Ralph Fletcher's short but sweet book, *A Writer's Notebook* (Fletcher 2003/2023). Inspired, I used printed pictures and my scrapbooking supplies to design the front and back cover of a spiral notebook. Using clear adhesive film, I covered both sides to protect them and happily showed my students. I then brought materials in for student writers to design their own covers as well.

With our first official writer's notebooks, I decided to use tabs like Ralph suggests. I chose a handful of sections and added little sticky flags onto the pages to make it easy to turn to those sections. Then, proud of myself for taking this step, I flipped through the empty pages. Eep! I realized that if my students were going to fill their notebooks, I would have to model how to do it. I would have to fill my own sections and be a writer with them. I remember how clearly this struck me. I had to walk the walk. This was when I reconnected with my writing identity.

After writer's workshop in middle school and high school, my writing became academic in college and stayed that way even after I started teaching—I wrote for my Master's and that was it. Now, I had my new writer's notebook, and I was keenly aware that I needed to pay attention to the world around me differently. I needed to not only laugh at something on the radio but remember it, so I could go and write it down. Things that struck an emotional chord stood out to me the most. Even over ten years later, I can remember things so clearly because I captured them in my notebook. Here's one example. In those days, I had students on my caseload in different schools, so I traveled to different locations throughout the day. The school day was already in full swing, and as I pulled into my next school, there was a van in front of me. A student got out with their backpack, and the van pulled away. I watched the student turn back to watch the van leave with a sort of listless feeling. Then, they slowly turned and walked into the building. The feeling of longing in the way that student looked back at the person who had dropped them off made me wonder: Were they sad? Were they disappointed? Were they sorry about something? It was one of the first times I remember wondering and letting my writing brain start to imagine and create a story.

It's amazing to me that over ten years later, I can go back to that page in my notebook and remember what I was thinking and feeling. I wrote it down because it mattered in the moment, but I can go back to it at any time for ideas. Having a way to collect ideas is imperative to living the life of a writer. It sends a clear message to students that they are writers because they have a way to collect their ideas and invites them into living the life of a writer. You can *tell* them that they are writers but *inviting* them into the action hits a bit differently.

Now that I'm teaching in a classroom setting, my students still design their notebook covers, and I will always love writers' notebooks, but my thinking about how writers collect ideas has evolved. I used to keep one personalized writer's notebook with tabs for different sections. Then, I shifted to smaller Moleskine notebooks that I could easily carry around in my purse. At some point, I craved having multiple notebooks for different projects. When I started blogging, I realized how the pictures and videos in my phone could help me remember what had happened that I wanted to write about—both for my family blog and for my teaching blog. Researching Doroteo Flores, the first Latino man to win the Boston Marathon, took me to the Boston Public Library where I found myself printing out copies of microfiche. I bought myself a plastic envelope to keep everything in as I worked on a nonfiction picture book biography about him. After I completed the first draft of my first young adult novel, I discovered *Save the Cat!* by Blake Snyder (Snyder 2005) and how it helps fiction writers outline the beats of their stories. I bought notecards and laid them out at a coffee shop to help me plan my revision and also to plan my next novel.

All of these count as ways to collect ideas! There are endless possibilities. In this chapter we'll look at options for you and your students to explore as you step into living the life of a writer.

A Moment To Reflect

Since our goal is to guide students to exploring what living the life of a writer looks like for them, we should be aware of what living the life of a writer looks like for us. Take some time to think about what writing *you* most typically do and make a list. This can include work-related emails to parents, your newsletter, lesson plans, and report card comments as well as writing you do outside of school. Then answer the following questions:

- What does your writing life look like now?
- What kind of writing do you engage in?
- Is there other writing you have done in the past? Or would like to do now or in the future?
- When it comes to the writing you do, what are some ways you collect ideas?

Remember, there's no judgment and everything counts. The idea is to bring awareness to what you most often do, so you can understand what living the life of a writer looks like for you as you guide your students toward what works for them.

EXPLORING COLLECTING OPTIONS

Writers have a way to collect ideas but that can look different for different writers or for different genres or at different times of the year. Ultimately, we want students to understand that part of living the life of a writer is having a way to collect and store ideas. Writers need a place to capture ideas and try things out. They need a place to record their thoughts. A place that is waiting for them to fill it.

When I was a child, I had notebooks and diaries. I didn't think of them as writer's notebooks until I was an adult, but I was capturing ideas, writing my thoughts, and trying things out, and that's exactly what a writer's notebook is for. There are different ways to use notebooks with students. I have had them create notebooks with tabs, notebooks for reading and for writing, and one notebook for everything. I lean toward one notebook for everything because it affirms that reading and writing influence each other. As readers, we are soaking up good words and studying what writers do. We make sense as readers, and then we make sense as writers—but all of it goes into our notebook. When it's time for students to write, they can write in their notebooks, and everything is there. If students struggle to read their own writing, it's sometimes not productive to be writing by hand. Our intention about focusing on living the life of a writer is to help students—and any writer—discover what works for them, so in these cases, I offer the opportunity to use electronic options like speech to text or Google Docs to capture ideas. I also trust them to know for themselves what's best. Some other examples of how students might collect ideas for writing include: notebooks, Google Docs, sticky notes, Google Slides, sketchbooks, iPad drawing app.

Even though I give students options throughout the school year, we still personalize notebooks together at the beginning of the school year. This is meaningful for two reasons. First, it allows writers to take ownership of their notebooks by personalizing them. Second, it allows them to share who they are, what they are interested in, and what they care about. Living in a digital world makes it really easy to find images and design covers that match student personalities and preferences. Designing our notebooks is one of my favorite activities because it allows me to get to know my young writers and talk with them about their interests.

In the 2019–2020 school year, I had several students who loved to draw and preferred to draw rather than write. I support writers with this passion and invite them to incorporate drawing into their work or use it as a way to explore ideas before writing. Every school year, I have at least one or two students who carry around a sketchbook or are drawing whenever they have the chance, and I encourage this.

Ultimately, an invitation to start collecting ideas activates our writer's eye. Having a writer's eye means paying attention to the world with a little bit more intention. Writers observe. Writers notice. Writers capture ideas. Writers are on the lookout for ideas and this is their invitation to start collecting. Collecting is an important step as students embrace writing as a part of their identity.

Living the Practice: Personalizing Notebook Covers

If you decide to use notebooks with students, inviting them to customize their covers is a way to encourage ownership. First off, you will need to decide what kind of notebook you are going to use. Some teachers put composition notebooks or spiral notebooks on the school supply list. I use Google Slides to set up a page that matches the size of students' notebooks. I then show my writers how I designed my cover and share the following criteria for success:

- Your first name in a big, bold font.
- At least seven images that represent you as a reader and a writer.
- At least one word or phrase that motivates you.

My notebook cover has the covers of books I like, images that represent my interests, and words that inspire me. Most students can get to work with this but sometimes I confer with students and help them brainstorm ideas. Oftentimes, students aren't sure what represents them as writers, so I will ask them what they care about or how they spend their time outside of school. I always point out how they might choose to write about those particular topics, so they definitely count as something that represents them as a reader and/or writer. This is a great activity for the beginning of the school year when I'm getting to know students and what they care about.

A writer's notebook is a safe space to try things out. You honor your students when you give them the opportunity to design their notebooks in ways that represent them.

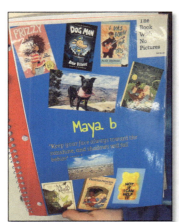 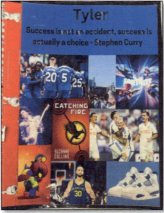 

Living the Practice: Question Storming to Activate Thinking

Whether you decide to use writers' notebooks, another way to collect ideas, or a combination, the next step is to activate students' thinking about how writers collect ideas. One way to do this is question storming. I discovered this idea from *A More Beautiful Question* by Warren Berger (Berger 2014). The book discusses the power of questioning to push one's thinking. Kids love to ask questions so this is a fun twist on brainstorming. Instead of brainstorming ideas, they make a list of questions they have. This usually gets their minds fired up, no matter the topic.

On your large format display, board, or a piece of chart paper, write the statement, "Writers have a way to collect ideas." Then ask students to only ask questions pertaining to this statement. You can model some examples

Writers Collect Ideas

Writers Have A Way to Collect Ideas

- Where do they collect ideas?
- Why do they collect ideas?
- What kind of ideas do they collect?
- How do they collect ideas?
- Do they collect in different ways?
- Do they organize their ideas?
- Is their collection physical or mental?
- Do some writers collect in a digital way?
- When do they collect their ideas?
- What do they do with their ideas?
- What do they do if they are stuck thinking of ideas?

Question Storming to Activate Our Thinking About the Practice of Having a Way to Collect Ideas

with them and then give them time to write as many questions as they can. Once you have a list of questions, compile them into one space. You can sort them as a class if you notice some trends in your students' questions.

Another option is to ask students to question storm around the practices of living the life of a writer presented in this book. Place large chart paper for each of the six statements around the room and have them gallery walk, writing questions for all of the tenets and posting them on the individual charts. Then you can revisit these questions as you introduce and zone in on each element.

Whether you decide to do one tenet at a time or all of them, ask students how they would answer these questions for themselves. Invite students to write long about what collecting looks like for them as a writer. Another option would be to have students interview each other. They can ask questions and share their ideas orally before writing their long-form response.

Remind students that exploring what it means to live the life of a writer is ongoing. You will continue to revisit what it looks like to collect ideas throughout the year and it might change from project to project. Your writers might explore and discover new ways of collecting as the year progresses and they work on different pieces. Talk to them about how every time we show up to the page, we are a different version of ourselves. Sometimes one way of collecting will work, other times it won't. Invite your writers to stay open to new ideas. The goal is for them to write, write, write, and having a range of options when it comes to collecting is important. Know and trust that there are ideas out there that will work for your students.

SETTING OURSELVES UP FOR SUCCESS

No doubt you've encountered your fair share of students who'll say, "I don't know what to write about!" This happens all the time. Even as writers practice looking out for ideas, sometimes they still need help.

I take great care to spend time helping students brainstorm ideas so whenever this happens, I direct them back to their writer's notebooks or wherever they have been collecting their ideas. I remind them that they have ideas and stories to share. This is a continuous attitude we need to take as teachers. Strong writing teachers are constantly sending messages to student writers that they *can* do this. We set them up to be successful and if they forget, we remind them. From their notebook covers to brainstorming lists to idea generating exercises, give students lots of options for finding something they can write about.

Sometimes students don't trust that they have the ideas or that the ideas that they have are worthy. When this happens, consider ways you can direct them back to themselves. They *do* have it in them. I don't have the answers. But I do have questions to help them find their own way. This was a mindset shift for me, and some students are more open to this than others. It's even empowering to know that I'm not here to give them all the answers, I'm here to help them find the answers for themselves. This is my ultimate goal. This is truly our work as teachers. Everything we do is in service to growing student independence. Whether it's independence as a learner or independence as a citizen or independence as a creator.

Throughout the year, I offer different exercises to help students brainstorm ideas. We collect ideas as we go and any time across the school year, I might encourage writers to dip back into their collection system to look for ideas. We want writers to be independent but even adult writers enjoy some guidance to help them unlock ideas they have inside them. We all have stories inside of us, but a large part of living the life of a writer is being intentional about giving those ideas attention, so we can bring them out into the open and onto the page.

Living the Practice: Using Mentor Texts for Idea Generation

I always start the school year with a read aloud. My absolute favorite picture book for the first day of school is *The Day You Begin* (Woodson 2018) written by Jacqueline Woodson and illustrated by Rafael Lopez. First, I read the book, and then, I reread it and we look for inspiration for ideas that we might write about.

Mentor texts are any text that can influence your own writing and incorporating them into your writing instruction empowers students in countless ways. I'll come back to mentor texts in Chapter 4 when we talk about strategies writers know, but it's worth looking at them here through the lens of idea generation.

Invite your students to open up to a blank page in their notebooks or their preferred collecting method. As you read your selected mentor text, pause and share a few ideas you notice that might inspire writing, and then invite your students to share any ideas they notice.

For example, I prepare our *The Day You Begin* read aloud by helping students connect to that first-day-of-school feeling when you walk into a new school or classroom. Then I write this on a piece of chart paper and invite them to write it down too, saying, "We could all write about our first day of school."

Next, I point out that the main character lives in a city. I share that I have never lived in a city but I could write about where I live. We add this to the list. Then, I continue reading, encouraging students to chime in as we continue to add to our list.

Any mentor text can be used to generate ideas like this, so you can adapt this idea easily. If it's not the first day of the school year, or you aren't planning to read *The Day You Begin*, try this with whatever text you are using in your classroom and see what possibilities your students discover.

Ideas from *The Day You Begin*

- Walking into a new place
- Place where you didn't fit in
- Your skin color
- Your clothes
- Your hair
- Being laughed at
- Moving
- Speaking a different language
- What is home to you
- Teacher
- Where you have traveled
- A place where you haven't felt good enough
- Souvenirs
- Feeling jealous
- Family
- Taking care of someone
- Lunch at school
- How your family makes different food (rice)
- Feeling left out
- How you have courage
- Felt included
- When you have shared your story
- Made a friend
- A time with reading

A List of Ideas for Writing After Reading *The Day You Begin* by Jacqueline Woodson and Rafael Lopez as a Mentor Text

Living the Practice: Lists for Idea Generation

Ask students to open up to a blank page in their notebooks or their preferred collecting method. Then give them some topics for lists. For instance, building off of the idea of writing about the first day of school from *The Day You Begin*, you might invite them to make a list of firsts—the first time they rode a bike, went swimming, visited the library, went to a sporting event, played a game. I follow the I do, we do, you do model with exercises like this. I share a couple of examples, ask them to share a few that we can add to our anchor chart, and then I encourage them to chat with an elbow partner while they continue to add to their personal lists while I circulate and chat with them. After writers have had time to discuss and add to their list, I invite them to share some of their ideas with the class. From moving around the room, I have an idea of people to call on or specific work to highlight.

To contrast a list of firsts, invite students to write a list of lasts. The last time they went to the park or a favorite restaurant, the last time they saw a loved one or wore a favorite article of clothing. This can bring up some emotional topics. There is value in writing about things that are close to our hearts. I often use this as an opportunity to be vulnerable here and share a story that comes to mind for me. Students are looking to us to be the lead writer in the room, so have a few ideas you're willing to share with students that might tug at their heartstrings. There's no right or wrong way to generate lists. Lists are accessible. Students don't have to write much. They are a great entryway to living the life of a writer because it's low stakes to write down a handful of potential ideas to write about.

You can spend time generating a bunch of lists at once or spread these out. Here are some other list ideas to try with your writers:

- important people in my life,
- places I have visited,
- things in my room/locker/backpack,
- prized possessions,
- things that scare me/creep me out/make me cringe,
- things I'm good at,
- favorites—sports, music, food, restaurants, books, famous people,
- hobbies/interests.

Living the Practice: Heart Maps for Idea Generation

I don't claim to be an expert when it comes to heart maps (you can look at what Georgia Heard (Heard 2016) has shared in her book about heart maps) but here's one way to create them with students.

Ask kids to open to a blank page in their notebooks or something that they can write/draw in/on. Invite them to draw a shape that takes up the entire page. This can be a heart or another shape. I model with a heart on my page but students can decide what shape they want. Then ask students to fill their shape with everything that matters to them. They can write, draw, or do a combination of writing and drawing. Encourage them to fill their shapes. As needed, offer some ideas for them to think about:

- favorite people, places, things, experiences,
- things that make you feel happy, sad, mad, annoyed, nervous,
- what you love,
- what you worry about.

Heart maps become a great tool when it comes to looking for ideas. Ideally, everything in their heart map is something that they can write about no matter what genre of writing they are working on. This is a great exercise at any time of year.

Living the Practice: Free Writing for Idea Generation

My all time favorite strategy for writers is free writing. I'll share more about it in later chapters, but I offer an introduction to it here as a way to collect or connect with ideas.

When you are ready to introduce free writing to your students, I suggest asking them to open to a blank page in their notebook or a fresh doc in whatever collection tool they are using. Then, I ask them to draw a giant X across the entire page. This is an idea from writer artist Lynda Barry in her book *What It Is* (Barry 2024). I like Barry's suggestion to draw an X across the entire page as a reminder to not take things too seriously. The page is not precious. The page is there to hold everything we have to share: the good, the bad, and the ugly.

After everyone has done this, model free writing in front of your students. Set a timer for one minute and either type so they can see what you are writing on your large format display or write with a document camera, so everyone can see what you're writing.

I have four rules for free writing that I share with students before I free write. I intentionally word these in a positive way so they know what to do.

1. Keep your hand moving.
2. Focus on ideas.
3. Let your ideas flow.
4. Be open.

When I introduce these, I take time to explain each a little bit. It's important to keep your hand moving because we are practicing building our stamina as writers and not overthinking things. Next, we focus on ideas, not spelling or capitalization or punctuation. This is just about finding ideas, so I tell them not to worry about anything else yet. When it comes to finding ideas, we have to let our ideas flow. We have to accept whatever ideas come to mind and let the ideas take us where we need to go. If they start writing about what they had for breakfast and end up writing about how weird the word banana is, so be it. Finally, I remind them

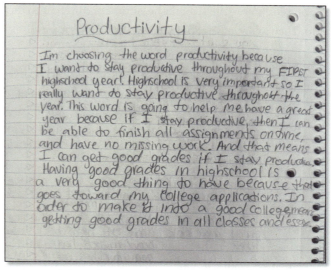

An Eighth Grader Free Writing About Her Word for the Year

to be open. This is not the time to judge our ideas in any way. Be open to whatever comes up, and write it down.

Make sure you really show them what this looks like as you model this. I start the one-minute timer and then take my free writing seriously. I make mistakes in spelling, don't bother to capitalize, leave off punctuation, let my ideas wander, and write fast. By the time one minute is up on the timer, I can see that I've added ideas to the page. Every time I do this, students end up reading aloud what I'm writing as I go and commenting about the mistakes I make or the silliness of some of my ideas. No matter, I make sure to show them how proud I am of my writing.

After you model for students, it's their turn! I always start with a one-minute free write so they can quickly find success. Sometimes I offer a topic to get them started; what they had for breakfast/lunch and/or what they are looking forward to for lunch/dinner is usually a universal topic that students can write into. But I also tell them they can write about whatever they want to write about. One minute goes fast but you—and they!—will be surprised at what they can write in only one minute. Celebrate with them when they are done and then challenge them to do it again, this time for two minutes. You can continue to grow their stamina for free writing over time and come back to this any time students need to get their ideas flowing.

A Moment To Reflect

You're doing it! Having a way to collect ideas helps writers jump right into living the life of a writer. Take a few minutes to check in with yourself again and acknowledge the emotions that are present now—these might be similar or different to how you were feeling in the Introduction. Then answer the following questions:

- What is your preferred way to collect ideas?
- How does it feel to have a way to collect ideas that is personal to you?
- How does this compare to what you have done (or were expected to do) to collect ideas in the past?

READY, SET, WRITE!

For me, having a place to collect ideas has been invaluable. Not long ago, my mom found one of my childhood notebooks and gave it to me. In it were some doodles and ideas and a note about how I loved to write so much. I could do it all day if I wanted to. Holding it and reading the words that young me wrote made me feel like I was holding a direct link to who I was then. Those ideas mattered then, enough that I saved that notebook. And those ideas matter now, knowing that I can still look back on them today and feel a connection.

A writer needs a space to collect their writing. To capture their thoughts. To record a seed idea. To explore possibilities. A space that is personal to them and that empowers them to boldly step into living the life of a writer.

Each practice in this book is an opportunity to explore what it means to live the life of a writer. We could have started anywhere but we started with how to collect ideas because having a container for ideas has a direct impact on our mindset and gets us ready to embark on the writing process. It sets us up to try different strategies, explore, and celebrate.

Do you feel the excitement building? You are ready. Your student writers are ready. You are helping them grow their understanding of what it means to live the life of a writer for themselves by starting with how they collect ideas. They are set to take the next step. Now that they have a way to collect ideas, we'll look at how we can support them as they take on or develop their writing identity. It's time to explore what it means to have a writer's mindset.

Writer's Affirmations

I have a way to collect all the stories so I can tell them when I'm ready. I know that I can express myself in my own way. I use pictures and words and feel empowered to write because I am a writer. I am a writer.

CHAPTER 2

Writers Have a Writer's Mindset

On a trip to Europe in the summer of 2024, my dad gazed up at the sky and said, "Is it me, or do the clouds seem closer here?" We were visiting the Palace of Versailles in France and I looked up too. Something about the entire sky felt bigger and the clouds did seem closer.

"Maybe it's because the sky is so open here?" I wondered aloud. In front of the palace, there aren't any large trees so when I marveled at the sky, nothing blocked my view. There was only a broad expanse of blue sky with puffy white clouds floating by.

I don't really think the clouds were closer to us in France than where we live in Illinois, but I do think that traveling encourages us to look around and notice more, or at least, to notice differently. Being a writer with a way to collect ideas works in much the same way. Having a way to collect naturally offers us an invitation to look more, to observe more, to notice more, to pay attention more.

There are stories everywhere. Our job as teachers is to help student writers be aware of the stories they have in their hearts and to impress upon them that their stories are worthy of being told. In Chapter 1, I shared options for ways to collect ideas and exercises for getting started. Setting up notebooks at the beginning of the year is a wonderful way to help students take ownership of their collecting and helps us get to know them and their interests, but there's another purpose. Having a dedicated way to collect ideas sets us up to cultivate our writer's mindset. I truly didn't start to practice a writer's mindset as an adult until I designed my own writer's notebook with my students. This was also the beginning of my realization that I actually wasn't teaching writing, I was teaching writers. In this chapter, I'll share what it means to have a writer's mindset and how to foster this in our student writers.

A Moment To Reflect

One of the most important things I want students to know is that they are writers because they write. You don't need to have a published book to be a writer. And, guess what? *You* are a writer too. You write—even if it's emails to parents or the newsletter you send home or report cards. You write.

We all have different ways of looking at our writing lives. For some, it's easy to feel like a writer and for others, it is hard to be able to say, "I am a writer." Wherever you fall on this spectrum, it's important to be aware of how you see yourself. Pause right now to journal about how you feel about being a writer. Use these questions to guide you:

- Is being a writer already part of your identity?
- Do you claim a writing identity or do you not quite feel like you can call yourself a writer? What has contributed or currently contributes to this?
- What has made it easy or hard to claim a writer's identity?

Continue to contemplate how you feel about yourself as a writer and what contributes to this mindset. Notice any shifts in your thinking as you continue to read and share what it means to live the life of a writer with your students.

TO HAVE A WRITER'S MINDSET

Having a writer's mindset means three things. First of all, it means using our writer's eye to actively pay attention and notice the world in order to write about it. Second, having a writer's mindset means identifying oneself as a writer. And finally, a writer's mindset means having a growth mindset that helps us navigate our writing process. These all go hand in hand because the more you look, observe, notice, and pay attention, the more ideas you collect. The more ideas you collect, the more you have to write about, the more confident you become in navigating your writing process. Ultimately, the more you write, the more you (hopefully) feel like a writer. After all, writers are people who write.

Humans tell stories, real and imagined, all the time. It's part of who we are.

I'm sorry I was late. I got caught by a train.

I went to the library and saw a painting that reminded me of a time in kindergarten.

I saw a real bear in the woods. No, I'm kidding. But that would have been cool.

Throughout our day we tell stories to those we meet whether we realize it or not. Bringing our awareness to this is part of living the life of a writer. Writers not only know that stories are all around them, but they actively look for them and notice specific details. There are stories all around us. Writers know this and actively pay attention not only to the stories but to the details that help them relay the stories effectively.

As a teacher, I'm also aware of my role in helping students develop this awareness. Sometimes a student is telling a story or describing something and I help them bring their awareness to the stories they are telling or how they are telling something that is unique to them. In supporting them in this way, we help them grow their awareness.

Additionally, writers take on a growth mindset as they navigate their writing process. Being aware of the fact that writers write and that writing means making progress through our process is important. We will spend more time exploring, understanding, and trusting our writing process in later chapters.

All the while, we affirm students' identities as writers. Do not underestimate this. When we continually remind them that they are in fact writers, we instill in them the foundational understanding that can navigate their writing process. As we'll see in later chapters, there are a myriad of different ways to move through the writing process, just like there are a myriad of different ways to be a writer. Inviting students to rightfully claim their writing identity is a powerful gift.

I SPY WITH MY LITTLE WRITER'S EYE

You and your student writers will continue to collect ideas as we explore how to engage our writer's eye. Maybe you are familiar with the phrase, "Show, don't tell." A writer's job is to capture a moment and describe it in such a way that it brings that moment to life for a reader. Whether writing fiction or nonfiction, putting the reader in the moment is imperative. The more we capture details in the moment, the more descriptive we can be and those details help to set our writing apart, help readers visualize, and ultimately, make our writing shine. But how can a writer do this if they are not actively paying attention in the first place?

This is where a writer's eye comes into play. Having a writer's eye means taking note of not only the details we see but also how they play into the entire scene. A writer needs to be aware of all their senses, including dialogue they hear, how people move, how all of this makes them feel, and what it might mean to themselves or others. At the same time, a writer is zooming in and out and contemplating. We think about what the reader needs to visualize the scene or moment. Reading and writing go hand in hand and this is an opportunity to explicitly help student writers make this connection. As readers, we use all the information the writer is giving us along with our experiences to make sense of what we are reading. As a writer, we think about what moves we make that will support the reader's understanding. Audience comes up a lot in my conferences with students. I will often point out what my writers are doing that helps their reader and offer ideas for them to consider that might make their ideas more clear to a reader. This is all part of taking on a writer's mindset. The writer pays attention in order to be intentional about the experience they are creating for the reader.

Humans tell stories all the time. We naturally identify stories to tell, whether it's something surprising that happened during the day, something that makes us laugh, or something that makes us annoyed, angry, or sad. Engaging a writer's eye means we notice these stories and capture them in our notebook or other collection system.

Most student writers recognize that to write, they need something to write about. Whether it's deciding what is worth writing about or coming up with a topic, writers need to make a choice. Oftentimes this stops writers, or rather, it keeps them from getting started easily. But this is why adopting a writer's mindset matters so much. Well before a writer decides that they are going to write—even before they decide they are a writer—they make a choice to think about what they might write about. Again, we can choose to write about something we know or we can imagine something, but making that decision is an important first step.

Once we have our notebooks or other collection system set up, I tell student writers that now we get to fill it. And, to do so, we must turn on our writer's eye. We bring awareness to our life when we live it by thinking about what we want to write about. In Chapter 4 we'll discuss strategies, but for now, the invitation is to start noticing. To start navigating through our days with a writer's mindset. This means paying more attention to what happens during the day and what details stand out.

For example, one day at school, the social worker was wearing an all pink dress. I didn't think much of it until I saw her at the end of the day when she was on her way to her car. Not only was she wearing the pink dress, but her phone case was pink, and her water bottle was pink. I have no idea what this means, if I'll ever actually write about it, or why it really matters other than it stood out to me, but I wrote it into my notebook, adding it to a collection of future writing fodder.

As we go about our daily lives, our writer's mindset nudges us to stay aware of what details stand out to us that we would include if we were going to write about a specific moment. Challenge yourself and your students to use your writer's eye to notice seed ideas throughout the day but also to capture details about those moments. This takes intention and practice, but when you and your students practice using your writer's eye, you'll start to see stories all around you. The beauty of this is that when it's time to write, you and your student writers won't have to sit and wonder what to write about, your collection of ideas will offer a plethora of options to choose from.

Living the Practice: Daily Diary to Collect Ideas

Ideally, writers notice an idea and capture it in their notebook right away. That's not always possible or plausible, so I suggest building in time during class to reflect on the day and identify meaningful moments to write about with your students. In this way, you are modeling what it looks like to live with a writer's mindset and also showing them the importance of this practice when it comes to living the life of a writer.

One of my favorite reflection exercises comes from Lynda Barry and her book *Syllabus* (Barry 2014). She calls it Daily Diary. On a piece of chart paper or on a blank piece of paper with a document camera, draw a vertical line down the middle of the page. Then draw a horizontal line about ⅗ of the way down the page. Now label the two columns in the first row, "Saw" and "Did." Label the two columns in the second row, "Drawn" and "Heard." Invite students to do the same. Think aloud as you reflect on the day and everything you have done in the last 24 hours. In the box that you labeled "Saw" make a list of seven things you saw. In the box that you labeled "Did" make a list of seven things that you did. Then draw something that you saw during the day. This should be a simple sketch. Finally, write a bit of dialogue you heard during the day. What you draw and the dialogue you capture could relate to or match what you shared in your lists of things you saw and did.

A Student Reflects on His Day Using a Daily Diary Notebook Entry

You can complete this as a class and ask students to help you brainstorm or you can model what this looks like and then have student writers try this on their own. This is a great time to remind students that when writers are collecting, the goal is to just get ideas down. They might want to write about some of these ideas or they may never choose to write about them, but writers collect ideas so they'll have writing topics to choose from, and you never know what might inspire you in the future.

WRITING WITH THE FIVE SENSES

Now that you've been collecting ideas, it's time to explore some of them a little more. Having a writer's mindset means using our writer's eye to be on the lookout for stories and also paying attention to details. Incorporating our five senses is a way of writing that brings our ideas to life for our readers.

I often use my phone as a way to collect ideas because it's simple and effective. Later, I'll go back and use a photo to put myself back into the moment and to start to develop a scene. One evening, I was out for ice cream with friends and the Miley Cyrus song *Party in the USA* came on in the shop. The teenagers behind the counter started singing the lyrics and dancing with each other. It was adorable, and I loved their enthusiasm and energy. I snapped a picture of my ice cream cone with them in the background because I wanted to remember the moment, but also, because I recognized that there was a seed idea for a story there. Summer, ice cream shop, teenagers, young love, music, dancing…that's the making for a young adult novel if I ever saw one!

Now I can pull up that photo and write about it using the five senses: the sweet smell of fresh waffle cones, seeing the sign of ice cream flavors hand written in pink chalk, hearing the beat of a song that made me want to dance, seeing heads bopping as the workers sang along, feeling the cold ice cream on my tongue, tasting the blue ice cream that reminds me of summer and my sister. I can do this with any seed ideas I've captured, whether that means going through my camera roll, going through my notebook, or going through the sticky notes in my desk drawer. Using our writer's eye to mine sensory details is a great way to bring the observations in our collections to life.

We're asking our student writers to activate their writer's mindset by noticing stories but also by asking them to notice details. We use our senses to navigate the world around us but writers have a heightened awareness of these senses so they can incorporate them into their writing.

Living the Practice: Using Sensory Details

Let's try using sensory details to describe a scene with your student writers! There are options for how you can do this. You can display a photo you took during class or invite students to bring a photo to write about.

With your writing and the photo on display where everyone can see, write the name of each of the five senses down the left side of the page. Invite students to do the same in their notebooks. Take time to model thinking of each of the senses while making a list of ideas within each of the five senses to describe the image. Model jumping from one sense to another, looking closely at the photo, and jotting down whatever comes to mind. You can invite students to offer ideas as well. Then have them try this on their own with an image of their choice.

The idea here is to model focusing your writer's eye with more intention in a way that continues to activate our writer's mindset. As students become more comfortable with this process, you'll notice that they'll organically start to capture specific sensory details they want to remember in their own notebooks.

Living the Practice: Flex Your Writer's Eye

Practice using your writer's eye and capturing sensory details by taking your student writers on a walk with their notebooks after reading "Instructions on Listening to Trees" by Mahogany L. Browne from the poetry collection *Woke: A Young Poet's Call to Justice* (Browne et al. 2020).

Read the poem and invite students to notice what sensory details Browne includes in the poem. You can also talk about what sound devices or figurative language she uses to bring the poem to life.

Then, take your students on a walk inside the school or outside. Show them how you were inspired by the poem to write a poem about your school. Ask student writers to notice what stands out to them and to write it down. Walk and write. Don't judge anything, just write it down. They should write down what they see but also include other senses. Encourage them to look at details or specific descriptions that bring the moment to life and write those things down too. Once you're back in class, ask students to share their notes with a partner and then share them out with the class. As a shared writing opportunity merge everyone's contributions (or invite them to submit one line via a Google Form) merging them together as a collective poem. Once completed, publish the piece by printing it and hanging it in your room where everyone can see it. You can even ask students to illustrate it.

Like any true community
We must nourish and care for one another
If we are to grow

We must listen when others talk
And listen when a question is asked

We show each other respect
And reflect on our actions

And this is when we remember that we are Bannockburn Bulldogs
The way....
The way...
The way...

We are part of someone else's journey
That's the way communities are built
Each root sprawling toward the edge of an infinite smile

A Shared Writing Poem Inspired by "Listening to Trees" by Mahogany L. Browne

CREATING A COMMUNITY OF WRITERS

Throughout history, writers have often been considered tortured souls. Sports columnist Red Smith is known for saying, "You simply sit down at the typewriter, open your veins, and bleed." But this doesn't have to be the case. Being part of Teachers Write has shown me that writing in community is a powerful experience. We can offer a similar experience for our students—a community of writers who support each other, share ideas and strategies, offer feedback, and celebrate each other. Shared writing, as we just explored, is one way to grow community while also giving student writers an opportunity to enhance their writer's mindset.

The more we practice looking for stories, the more easily we will be able to spot them. Students naturally come to class sharing stories and this is a great way to connect them to their writer's mindset. I pay attention to the stories they tell or the things that happen in class. I will often confer with a student and say, "That's a story!" Or when it's time to generate ideas, I refer back to their shared stories to show student writers the options they have. Megan Stielstra, one of my favorite essayists and writing teachers, would often stop me or others in class and say, "Write that down!" She especially did this when she heard something that stood out to her. It has stuck with me. I've gotten better at keeping my eyes and ears peeled for when others say something that just hits, helping writers see how it could turn into a line in a story or the title of an essay. This comes with practice. When you are paying attention, there are stories all around you. And being part of a writing community that reminds us of this further helps us develop our writer's mindsets.

I also use an activity called Writer's Circle to share stories as a community and bring our awareness to the fact that we all have stories to tell and ideas to share. In my class, we move tables out of the way and arrange chairs in a circle, so everyone is facing each other. I sit in the circle with students and invite any other adults in the room to join as well. After sharing the purpose of a Writer's Circle and going over our norms, I post a prompt specific to writing on a large format display. Sometimes I add a sentence stem to help them organize their thoughts. We have a stuffed animal that we pass around the circle, and only the person holding it talks. Everyone else listens. Each person has an opportunity to share or pass and we go around the whole circle.

Language Arts is, after all, a humanities class. In Circle, we share writing ideas, but we also talk about what works for us, what we do if we get stuck, what we're working on in general. Sometimes students bring their notebooks and we gather ideas on chart paper and in our notebooks. In listening, students hear that there are different options for stories to tell, for opinions to have, and for ways to navigate the writing process. This is an activity that works for so many different reasons and one that I find is meaningful in an academic way and also in a social-emotional way.

Living the Practice: Writer's Circle

To facilitate the Circle Process with your students, I suggest talking about what and why before inviting your students to move into a writer's circle.

Start by displaying understandings and agreements the students need to be aware of when participating in a Writer's Circle and going over them in detail. This is something you can co-create with your writers, but I find that giving them to students at first is helpful because they may not be familiar with Circle Process. Later, you can revise or design your own once they have experience with a Writer's Circle.

Understandings

- The facilitator guides the process
- Speak only when you have the talking piece
- Speak for up to two minutes
- You have the option to pass
- Be present in the moment and listen
- Listen with an open heart and honor their truth
- Feel whatever emotions come up
- Respect confidentiality
- Remember to breathe

Agreements

- Speak from the heart
  - only when you have the talking piece
  - authentic contributions
- Listen from the heart
  - without judgment
  - with compassion
  - Speak spontaneously
    - spend time listening
    - not thinking about what you're going to say
  - Speak leanly
    - be aware of your time
  - What is shared in the circle stays in the circle

Once you have gone over understanding and agreements, ask them why they think it might be beneficial to participate in Writer's Circle. Write students' answers down and add your thinking to theirs as you do.

Why do we do circle?

- Get to know other people's thoughts
- Practice letting people talk and not talking over them
- Time to unwind at the end of the week
- Speaking - sharing your thinking about a topic

Next, ask them to share why this is something to take seriously. I always tell my students that they might feel that I'm extra firm when it comes to Writer's Circle and that is for a very specific reason. Asking this question helps them understand the importance of being a respectful member of the Writer's Circle.

> ## Why do we have to take it so seriously?
>
> - It's important to let people who don't feel heard speak
> - Everyone gets a chance to share
> - Practicing being respectful to others
> - It helps people feel safe to share

The first question I suggest asking is, "How does it feel to be in a circle like this?" Over the years, I've learned that this can actually feel awkward for some students. Middle schoolers, for example, are often self conscious and worry that everyone is looking at and judging them, so to sit in front of each other like this can feel very vulnerable. Once everyone has had the chance to share, remind them of the agreements and talk about what to do if they start to feel nervous or if they get the giggles. It happens quite a lot so it's helpful to talk about what to do. Teach them to look at their shoes or look at the ground or look at their hands instead of looking at each other and to breathe. Then practice this together.

After that, move into a question on a topic that will engage their writer's mindset. It can be a get-to-know-you question or something related to school. It can be asking them to share a memory or something about themselves. Here are some possibilities for Writer's Circle questions:

- What has been your favorite grade in school and why?
- Who is an adult in your life who means a lot to you? What value or lesson have you learned from them?
- If you could travel anywhere in the world, where would you visit and what would you eat there?
- What do you say to yourself if you are feeling stuck?
- How has technology helped you overcome a weakness?

When you are done, pass the talking piece around one more time and ask each student to say, "I commit to respect the circle." This is a way to end Circle that reminds everyone of the understandings and agreements of Circle.

A WRITER'S MINDSET IS A GROWTH MINDSET

It was a Saturday morning in January of 2020, and I was about twenty minutes into our day-long hike up to the top of Volcán Tacana, the second tallest volcano in Central America at over 13,000 feet. My cousin Edgar, an adventure guide in Guatemala, was leading a group to the top where we would spend the night in a dried up crater and then hike to the peak to watch the sunrise in the morning.

I had already taken off my long sleeve shirt and tucked it into my backpack. I had already stopped to drink water. I had already been passed by all the other hikers in our group. I was hot and out of breath and in over my head.

Like a writer who starts to work on a piece and realizes they need a variety of strategies to help them through, I was already making adjustments. Was I going to turn around and go back? No, that wasn't an option. My only choice was to figure out how to slow my breathing, stop worrying about comparing myself to others, and get myself up this volcano. I focused on taking one step at a time.

Stepping right.

Stepping left.

Stepping right.

Stepping left.

Slowing down my pace allowed me to also slow my breathing and to get into a rhythm. It wasn't a race, it was about staying in the game. I told myself over and over again that I was doing it. Every step was evidence that I was, in fact, climbing that volcano.

Writers must embrace a growth mindset much like I did on the volcano. Not only did I make adjustments based on my skills as a hiker, but I made adjustments to my mindset. Writing can bring up a wide array of emotions. Past experiences might bolster us or undermine us. Similarly, getting to the end might seem daunting or overwhelming. We can support our students by showing them ways to move forward with their writing while also affirming their efforts. Sometimes giving students one small element to focus on helps them move forward. Sometimes giving them confidence in their abilities helps them move forward. Part of being a teacher of student writers is being aware that both are needed when helping student writers embrace a growth mindset.

Taking on a growth mindset means knowing and trusting that, even if it feels hard, we can grow as writers. We can face challenges, find a way to move forward despite obstacles, learn from feedback, be inspired by other writers, and embrace effort and progress.

It was early evening when I finally made it up to the crater. I was the very last person, and I was exhausted. I couldn't see the rest of the group, and the trail was hard to make out, but my cousin came back to walk with me for the last part. I was so tired that Edgar helped me pitch my tent. I crawled right in, falling asleep without eating dinner. Every muscle ached, but I made it.

In the morning, it was dark and cold as I scrambled up the rocky peak with only the light from my headlamp, but it was worth it to be above the clouds and on top of the world as the sun rose. And I knew I was a backpacker. How could anyone argue otherwise?

While our job as teachers is to teach our students how to write, we also have a responsibility to help them step fully into their identity as writers. By the end of their time with us, students should know that they are writers. How could anyone argue otherwise? After all, writers write.

Living the life of a writer is arduous. It entails a lot. While it's not as physically demanding as hiking to the peak of a volcano, it is still a challenge and it does require an element of mental fortitude. Writing is not just something we do, it is part of who we are.

In her book, *In Pictures and Words,* Katie Wood Ray writes, "With blank paper in front of them, students have to learn how to make *something* out of *nothing*, and they must learn to come back the next day and do it again" (Ray 2010, 21).

Facing a blank page is something all writers have to do. This is at the heart of writing. You have a blank page…and then you don't. When you've added words or pictures to a page, you are writing. I come back to this with students again and again as I nudge them toward confidence in themselves as writers. Sometimes it's about putting one word down and then another.

Stepping left.

Stepping right.

And while it is about finding or recognizing what to write about, it is also about knowing how to motivate ourselves to stay the course. As teachers, our job is to remind student writers that they can do it again and again, but it is also our job to help them discover how they can do this for themselves by exploring what living the life of a writer means to each of them.

A Moment To Reflect

Humans are resilient. We find ways to persevere. This serves us in living the life of a writer. Pause now to think about a time in your life when you needed to find a way to persevere and to be resilient and write about it by answering the following questions.

- What did you go through?
- What helped you get through that experience?

- What resources did you call on to help you?
- How might you apply what you learned to living the life of a writer?

Just like my volcano hike, consider hard things you have done in your life and how you've learned from practices that have worked for you in the past. You are your best teacher. For instance, while I appreciate words of encouragement from friends and family, I know what messages I need to hear to help myself in different situations. Just like I had a mantra when I climbed the volcano, having a writer's mindset means we find ways to motivate ourselves and keep going. We can support this in students by helping them identify words or phrases that empower them in living the life of a writer.

WORDS OF ENCOURAGEMENT AND HABIT LOOPS

Let's return to the idea of free writing but reframe this practice as a way to support students in growing their writer's mindset through words as encouragement.

I discovered this opportunity at a writing retreat held by Brenda Power, the founder of Choice Literacy, a digital publication for educators. She spread cards with empowering words and phrases on them all around the room. The other writers and I were invited to walk around and look for words that called out to us or were inspiring to us. I chose two that I liked a lot. One said, "I'm a writer. I can write. The proof is on the page." Those words really spoke to me because I was still growing my confidence as a writer. Viewing the words on the page as proof that I am a writer felt really validating. After all, writers write, and I was writing. The other card I chose read, "Bring it on, blank page!" I really liked this one because it also helped me feel more confident as a writer. Writers show up and have to face a blank page again and again so this made me feel that I was up to that challenge. I still feel empowered and fierce and ready to write each time I read it.

At this same retreat, Brenda had also given us a book called *The Power of Habit* by Charles Duhigg (Duhigg 2012). In *The Power of Habit*, Duhigg explains that humans run on habits and routines and spends a chapter talking about habit loops which consist of a cue, a routine, and a reward. I decided developing a habit loop for my writing life would be beneficial. Since I was working on drafting my novel, I knew the behavior I wanted to increase was free writing. Next, I thought about what I could use to cue my free writing habit. When I sit down to write, especially to free write, I now say to myself, "Bring it on, blank page!" Sometimes I take a deep breath or take off my jewelry and my watch and then I set a timer and write. When the timer goes off, I pause and look at my page and say to myself, "I'm a writer. I can write. The proof is on the page." This is my simple habit loop that I can do anywhere at any time and doesn't require anything but me. Over the years, this habit has served me really well because I know when I say, "Bring it on, blank page!", my brain is ready to go.

Having a writer's mindset that motivates us is imperative and we need to teach students how to take care of themselves by developing a positive mindset while writing. Now, when I first introduce free writing to students, I share my habit loop with them and we use my habit loop to free write together. I encourage students to say, "Bring it on, blank page!" with me. We bring a lot of energy to this, and the cheesier I am, the more free students feel to join in along with me. While students are writing, I walk around the room and see how they are doing. If a writer is stuck, I will remind them that they can just write a word or phrase until they come up with an idea. My goal is to make sure everyone has written something. When the time is up, I tell them to look over the page in front of them and then together, we say, "I'm a writer. I can write. The proof is on the page."

After students have tried my habit loop, I show them a short video about habit loops and how we can use them to help us mind our mindset. I explain my free writing habit loop by showing them my cue, routine, and reward. Then I display additional examples so that they can create their own in their notebooks. This always incites a great discussion about positive self-talk and what kinds of messages are most motivating to them. We talk about what adults, teammates, or coaches might say and how we can bring that energy into their writing life. Then, using words or images, they design a card for their cue and a card for their reward and share them with the class. Afterward, any time we free write, they use their own personalized free writing habit loop. I remind students that sometimes you just need to start writing and to get words out and that this method will help them to do that.

Creating free writing habit loops is one of my favorite things to do. It helps with our mindset as writers, it helps us embrace free writing, and it helps affirm our identities as writers. We're able to write more, to be more willing to take risks, to explore new ideas, to keep writing over time. There are lots of people who can give you ideas and strategies and exercises and feedback and all of that is great. But at the heart of it all is the writer, and empowering a writer to know themselves, to know what works for them, and to care for themselves through it all is the most important work we can do. When our students reflect on their writing life over the months with us, we want them to see how all the words on all the pages add up. We want them to celebrate their accomplishments. To know they are, in fact, writers. The proof is right there on the page.

Living the Practice: Free Writing Habit Loops

You can invite students to create their own free writing habit loops. Start by showing them a video about habit loops. I created this one that gives them a free writing example (Vincent 2025).

Habit Loops—Exploring a Writer's Mindset Video

Explain that they'll be deciding what message they need to hear as their cue and then another message they need to hear as their reward. Review the expectations for free writing again:

1. Keep your hand moving.

2. Focus on ideas.

3. Let your ideas flow.

4. Be open.

On your large format display, show students examples of words or phrases they can use as their cue. Invite them to find one that they like, combine multiple examples, or come up with something totally different on their own. They can write this in their notebook or you can invite them to create slides with images or a background to make it more fun. After they have all chosen what they want to say to themselves as a cue, display the examples for rewards. Give students time to choose or write their own reward statements. Once they have their habit loops in place, they can return to it any time they write. Some students might want to share their habit loops with an accountability partner or keep them as reminders with their writing supplies for easy reference.

A Moment To Reflect

Take some time to think about what words or phrases are empowering and uplifting to you and how you might craft those into your own habit loops for writing. Everyone is unique, and what works for me might not work for you. My goal in writing this book is not for you to teach exactly how I do. Instead, I want you to feel empowered to explore what living the life of a writer means for you and then to bring that to your work with student writers. Ultimately, I hope you feel more confident in teaching, conferring, and leading student writers.

TAKING BACK OUR POWER

Students want to know that they are doing things right, doing a good job, or meeting our expectations. Oftentimes, as writers tell me what they accomplished or show me something, I hear five familiar words, "Are you proud of me?" I love when kids share celebrations with me. It's exciting that they want to tell me and fun to cheer for them, but I try to connect this back to their writer's mindset by asking them, "Are *you* proud of *yourself*?" I want to remind them that their opinion is the one that matters most. It's great to be appreciated but only they know how truly awesome they are. And, even if they have people in their lives who see and value and appreciate them, it still needs to come from within. When we help writers design their own habit loops, we are not only celebrating them and their progress, but we are shifting their mindset toward celebrating themselves exactly how they need and want to be celebrated. That's a beautiful gift to give themselves.

POWERING THROUGH

Speaking of power, the work we have been doing to develop our mindsets and identities as writers and to foster that in our students is important foundational work that will help us navigate the writing process. Cultivating a writer's mindset matters because we are helping our student writers see that they are writers and writers work through a writing process. They are humans who notice and pay attention and use writing to make sense of the world and share their insight with others. We're in it for the journey, we're in it for the experience. Yes, we're working toward final products that we can share with others, but ultimately, we're working toward understanding our human experience. Each writer needs to figure out what works for them, how they do things, what it looks like for them to navigate the writing process.

As we invite students to see themselves as writers, they become more and more aware of what it looks like for them to live the life of a writer. Part of having a writer's mindset is being able to see yourself through the process. That means they now start to explore *their* process. Having a writer's mindset means needing to know what we do when a roadblock appears. *How do we make our way past it? Do we go around it? Do we sit and admire it for a bit? Do we bulldoze through it? Do we gingerly walk around it? Do we get someone to carry us over it? Do we demolish it?* There are so many options. Being able to see that we are always choosing what story we want to believe is such a big part of life. I could believe that I don't have enough time to write or I could believe that five minutes a day is enough time to write. I could believe that no one wants to read my words or I could believe that somewhere out there is a young Latina woman just like I was who would appreciate my story. I could believe that my words should come out perfectly the first time around or I could believe that revision is where we polish our words to make them shine. These are all stories and we can choose which we want to believe. It will take practice but when we release ourselves and our student writers from the distracting stories we've been told and, instead, shift our thinking toward more validating self-talk, it is empowering. It's all in our mindset. We can unleash our potential, to do exactly what we were born to do.

Caring for our mindset matters. We need to remember to be kind to ourselves. Capitalism and colonialism focus so much on productivity and how to benefit from the production or how to turn that production into something else that it's possible to worry so much about the writing and to forget about the writer. We have to be careful of this. When we exist in a system that wasn't designed for humans—from the students to the teachers to the administrators—we need to make sure that we take care of ourselves. This goes for writers of all ages and in all aspects of publishing. Living the life of a writer is beautiful. Just be careful not to get so caught up in the writing that you lose sight of you as the writer. This matters.

READY, SET, WRITE!

When I started writing my first novel, it took a while to believe in myself as a writer and to feel comfortable claiming that identity. The more I kept writing, the more confident I felt saying I was a writer. I would remind myself that writers write and I was definitely writing so I was a writer. The more I wrote, the more closely I thought about what I cared to write about. My young adult novels are about characters figuring out who they are and navigating growing up. My blog posts and articles for teachers are about what I value—meeting authors and illustrators, using mentor texts, developing a growth mindset, being anti-racist and anti-bias. Now, when I write essays, I explore my experiences and how they shape me. All of this writing helped me realize that writing is a form of identity work. In writing, you get to know yourself better. When we write, we bring attention to what matters to us and in doing so, we become aware of what matters to us. This awareness allows us space to think about how people, places, and experiences have shaped us.

My mindset has shifted in so many ways thanks to my writing practice. I notice the world differently, I notice how I show up in the world, I notice how I make decisions to move forward. I feel much more aligned in my choices now than ever thanks to my writing life. Our student writers can do this too. Help them interrogate where their current writing mindset might be holding them back and show them how to make intentional shifts in their thinking that will help them fully step into, celebrate, and live their writing life!

Writer's Affirmations

There are ideas all around me! I have so many stories to tell! Stories find me! I understand that stories are everywhere. I feel empowered in knowing that not only are there so many stories to tell but I get to tell them because I am a writer. I am a writer.

CHAPTER 3

Writers Know that Writing is a Process

I was making my way around the room to check in and confer with seventh-grade writers about their progress on their research-based information writing. In teams, students were participating in their First Lego League robotics competition, with each reading and annotating their resources in order to write an essay and contribute to their group's innovation project. Some students sat in flexible seating—we have couches, small armchairs, and beanbags. Others were huddled with their friends around a table. Xander was sitting on his own at a table with a computer in front of him. I sat down beside him and started to ask the questions I commonly use for conferring.

"How's it going?"

He was quiet at first as he contemplated his progress.

"Okay," he said.

I looked at his screen and he had a document open with a three column table on it.

"Can you tell me what you're working on right now?"

He pointed at his screen and started to explain how he was gathering information and sorting his research into three columns to compare the difference between acrylic paint, oil paint, and watercolor.

Earlier in the unit, I had introduced the students to using nonfiction signposts to read and annotate with an article from Newsela as an anchor text. Then I asked them to use the signposts while reading resources they found on their own based on their teams' topics. Never did I show them how to collect their thinking or mention using a table to organize their notes. But here was Xander taking the information and making sense of it in his own way.

Moments like this are so exciting as a teacher! I love to see students take ownership of the learning in this way. Now I had an opportunity to bring Xander's awareness to this choice and validate his process.

"So…what I asked you to do was to read and use the signposts to help you annotate. You're making meaning of what you're reading and organizing your research. I can see how this is going to help you when it's time to share your comparison of these types of paints."

He nodded.

I continued, "Is there a way you can add your thinking about each of the bullet points you have?"

"Yeah, I can add that under each one."

"Great! Is there anything I can help you with or are you good to keep going?"

Xander said he was good and I took that as my cue to move on to check in with other students.

Our job as teachers is to help student writers navigate the writing process and understand that writing is a process and that there are stages we move through toward a polished piece of writing. It's also important that we give student writers space to navigate a process that works for them with our guidance. This is something that's often forgotten in our writing curriculum. Grounded in their writer's identity and mindset, we can help students recognize that—though there is a generalized writing process—most writers eventually find a writing cadence that's individualized to their personal strengths and needs.

So far, we have explored two practices that set the foundation for living the life of a writer: a way to collect ideas and a writer's mindset. We will, of course, continue to revisit these with student writers throughout the school year, but now it's time to explore how we guide students through their writing process on a daily basis. In this chapter, we will show student writers that writing is a process by taking an inquiry-based approach. Essentially, we'll continually consider, *How do writers write?* This guiding question invites student writers to explore the myriad of ways they might answer it as they evolve their own writing process.

A Moment To Reflect

At this point, take a quick moment to free write about what comes to mind when you think of the writing process, both as a writer and as a teacher. Here are some questions to guide your reflection:

- What is your understanding of the writing process?
- What do you believe about the writing process?
- In your experiences as a student writer, did you learn about the writing process?
- As a teacher, do you teach your students about the writing process?
- What steps or stages of the writing process do you teach your students and what does this look like?

WRITING PROCESS WITH WRITER'S WORKSHOP

When I first started teaching back in 2002, I bought a set of writing process posters from the local teacher store. The stages of the writing process included in the set were: brainstorming, drafting, revising, editing, and publishing. At the time, I laminated them and happily put them up on the wall in my teaching space. After doing so much personal writing though, I've come to look at the writing process differently. Writers spend time in each of these areas, to be sure, but the writing process is not a linear process, and it's important that we make this clear to student writers.

We can guide student writers through the different parts of the writing process while also helping them find a process that works for them and for the particular piece they are working on at the time they are working on it. As I explore different genres of writing, I'm realizing more and more that my process for one piece might work just as well for another piece, or it might need to be different. Similarly, who I am when I show up to write might change over time. Sometimes I like to free write, so I can have something to work with, and other times, I like to have a clear structure before I start to write. Sometimes I need to do lots of research and lots of brainstorming and working with the information, and sometimes I write and pause to collect research as needed. Our students need to understand that this is how authentic writing happens. It's organic. Their writing process will adapt and adjust based on who they are as writers and the writing they are doing.

For example, a while back my sixth-grade writers were working on *Where I'm From* poems. My mini lessons offered options for them to create identity webs and then to choose one area from their identity web to turn into a list of ideas. I was walking around and Ingrid showed me her list of ideas about her siblings. Next to the ideas she had brainstormed, she had drawn lines to show how the ideas related to each of her siblings. She showed me what she did and asked if it was okay, and I told her it was exactly what she should be doing. While Ingrid was busy planning, another student, Abe, wanted to skip to typing right away. They each had their own way to start to explore their ideas and, of course, I encouraged that.

Knowing this, consider how we might give students space to explore their process. While they will most likely move from brainstorming ideas to drafting to revising to editing to publishing, giving them space to explore what each of these looks like for them at their own pace and to move back and forth within this structure is important in growing their confidence as writers. We are there to guide them and help them embrace progress over perfection as they find joy in the journey *and* as they develop their confidence in their ability to navigate their own writing process.

When it comes to teaching the practices students need to live the life of a writer, I prefer to follow a traditional model of writer's workshop, which offers a structure that ensures students have time to write while being in community with other writers. This includes a whole group mini lesson, time for independent writing, time to confer with writers, and time for sharing and celebrating our efforts. Establishing this structure allows me to introduce and explore the general stages of the writing process while giving student writers time to explore their process in community with myself and other writers in the room. Discussions with others help us grow our confidence, explore possibilities, and find momentum to keep moving forward through the writing process. I find that the structure of workshop gives students a safe space and lots of opportunities to figure out what living the life of a writer looks like for them throughout the year as we explore different genres of writing.

There is, after all, no one way to be a writer. I have read books about writing from authors like Stephen King, Natalie Goldberg, Anne Lamott, Julia Cameron, and Lynda Barry, and I have taken workshops with a variety of writers who share how they approach writing. Every one of them is a writer, but they have their unique ways of approaching the writing process. One of my favorite examples of this comes from Stephen King. In his book *On Writing* (King 2020), King explains how he used to write in his laundry room. I thought that was a neat idea, so I tried it myself. I wrote most of my first novel from the coziness of my laundry room. I would wake up early and sneak in there to write before my family woke up. It was warm and smelled good, and I loved the feeling of being in a snug space. It worked for me. Do I still write in my laundry room? Usually not. But there are times when I need to minimize distractions, and I might sneak in there to write. Is it conventional? Probably not. But it worked for Stephen King, and who's going to argue that he's not a writer?

A Moment To Reflect

I experienced writer's workshop as a student in middle school and high school so embracing its structure as a teacher made sense to me and came easily. You might be someone who experienced writer's workshop as a student like I did, or you might have had a mix of experiences. My junior year in high school, I had a very traditional teacher who lectured on the reading we were assigned—*A Portrait of the Artist as a Young Man* by James Joyce (1916/2024) and *Gulliver's Travels* by Jonathan Swift (1726/2022) were two of the books we read—and marked up the essays we wrote in response to the reading with red ink. That year helped me really see the contrast from learning in a writer's workshop versus in a traditional setting.

Reflect on your experiences in school when it came to how you were supported in working toward a finished piece of writing.

- Did you have time to write in class?
- Did you experience a workshop model?
- Did you receive feedback during the process?
- Did you confer with your teacher(s)?
- How did this impact you and your understanding of yourself as a writer?
- How did you feel about yourself as a writer?
- What writing processes were you taught?
- Were you encouraged to part from those processes and make them your own? How did this affect you as a developing writer?

THROUGH THE WRITING PROCESS

Within the structure of a writer's workshop, I guide students toward a finished piece that they will turn in to me as a summative assessment. I grade this using a checklist that the class establishes together at the beginning of a unit. This shows me how they navigate process writing. Before we start a unit, I give a pre-assessment which shows me how students do with on-demand writing and gives me information for planning mini lessons for 1:1 and small group work. At the end of each unit, I give a post-assessment which also includes on-demand writing. Since pre-assessment and post-assessment are similar, I can see how student writers have grown.

Reading the pre-assessment writing allows me to look at what student writers are able to do and where I need to focus my instruction. Keeping this in mind, I start to think about what student writers will need to move through the writing process toward a finished piece that shows what is expected on the checklist. This allows me to plan mini lessons that will give students examples of how to approach the writing they are doing and support them as they move through their writing process during independent work time.

While the process isn't always as linear as brainstorm, draft, revise, edit, and publish, it is in fact a process. We want to design mini lessons that give students opportunities to learn about moves that writers make, and then allow them time to try those moves in their own writing during independent work time and with our support.

Sometimes students will take an idea directly from what we discuss in our mini lesson, and other times, they won't. I've learned over the years that it's important to teach the mini lesson but it's also important to give students space to explore what they need and what works for them. As a teacher, I don't presume to have all the answers, nor do I stand at the front of the room and tell students to do things my way. Instead, I show student writers the common practices that writers engage in and invite them to engage in them as well.

I design mini lessons to give students things to consider, and then I release them to work. My goal is to grow their independence as writers. That means that during *brainstorming*, they need time to face the blank page and figure out how to navigate their process. We've already worked on establishing our writer's mindset and they can continue to use positive self-talk to move through their process. I'll also be conferring with them and checking in. And, of course, we'll generate lists with some options of what they can do to get themselves started, but I always tell students that they can do what makes sense for them. Trust is absolutely imperative to facilitating a writer's workshop. I trust that students will rise to the occasion and do what they need to do.

I constantly think about how the mini lessons I plan will give student writers support through the process. We usually start by reading a mentor text that we can use to launch our brainstorming. Then we look at organization and structure. From there I offer moves writers can make based on the genre. Here, I rely on standards and the checklists I create for students. Even as we work through the writer's workshop structure, I'm keeping my eye out for ways I can offer them guidance toward moving through their individual writing process.

COLLECTING

A student once wrote in her reflection that she was so excited to draft because she had been making lots of lists, and she was feeling ready to write. That's how writing should be! It should be fun! If we engage in collecting ideas, then things flow much more easily when it's time to go off and write about those ideas.

We have a writer's mindset and we use our writer's eye to collect ideas. We also engage in exercises in our notebooks to find ideas. Once we have some ideas gathered up, we can look at the different options and choose one to work with. Sometimes I coach student writers to choose an idea and go with it. They can always get started and switch if they decide to go with a different idea. Other times, student writers need time to narrow their options down or time to develop their thinking before they write. Ultimately, that is a learning experience in and of itself. I've had students tell me that they spent so much time not knowing what to do, and then they had to rush through the rest of their process. This is a great reminder that there isn't a right or wrong answer, there is only a choice that writers make and explore, which can stir great conversations about how doing so served them (or didn't) as well as an opportunity to reflect and plan for how they might want to adjust that part of their writing process for next time.

At this point, you're likely thinking of all the ways you teach students to collect ideas for their writing. Some of collecting can include planning and thinking about how to organize ideas. Keep in mind that these two need to allow for flexibility as students learn to use them in their own way. For instance, like me, you probably consider graphic organizers as an awesome scaffold for helping students collect ideas. Graphic organizers are an awesome way to visually represent ideas. I believe in offering examples of graphic organizers and sharing how they might be used, but I also believe in giving students choice in how to use them and when. It's rare for me to say that every student needs to have a Venn diagram or to complete an outline before they write. These are tools that are available to them as needed, and I certainly teach my writers how and when to utilize them, but I view graphic organizers as resources that are most effective when students choose to use them when their process calls them to do so.

Living the Practice: Webs

One option writers may want to include in their collecting process is webbing. While other strategies like creating a list don't have to be done in a specific order, a web lends itself to developing ideas around a topic while starting to organize those ideas a bit.

On chart paper or in a notebook that you are displaying with a document camera, draw a large circle in the middle of the page. Show students that you can use a web to brainstorm but also start to organize ideas preliminarily by writing the topic in the middle of the page. Then ask students to help brainstorm ideas and write those ideas on lines reaching out from the circle. I love to use webs to explore our identity at the beginning of the year. Having experience with this personal example of webbing makes it easy to then use a web later in writing to develop a character or to sort through information they want to share about a specific topic, writing a topic in the circle and then branching out from there to share what they know about it and breaking the topic even further down. Similarly, webs work well for argument writing in that students can write their claim in the middle and then branch out with the evidence points they would share to make their argument.

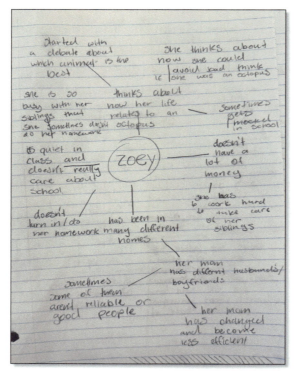

A Student Writer Uses a Web to Collect Her Thinking About a Character in a Book

Living the Practice: Stop and Jot

Actively responding to what we are reading is an opportunity to gather ideas for writing because these small stops along the way give us notes that we can come back to when it's time to write longer about what we have read. This can be an especially helpful addition to the writing process when writers are researching to gather notes to write an information piece or to identify evidence we might use to support an argument.

On a piece of chart paper or in a notebook that you are displaying with a document camera, draw a line down the middle of the page. On the left, label the column, "In The Text." On the right, label the column, "In My Head." Use your anchor text to read and model your thinking out loud for students. Share the thought and then write it down on the right column. Then copy over the text you responded to in the left column. Make sure to use quotation marks and explain that when you are citing a text, it's important to use quotation marks to show that you are directly quoting the text. Also include the page number, explaining that this will make it easy to come back to later. Continue to read and add entries as you go. Stop and Jot is a way for students to actively engage with the text, make their thoughts visible, and gather ideas that they can come back to later.

DRAFTING

At The Art Institute of Chicago there is a room where the painting *A Sunday on La Grande Jatte* by Georges Seurat hangs. It's one of the highlights of the museum. I took my cousin and her family there when they visited from Guatemala. While my cousin's husband took his time to study the painting and talk to his kids about the art, I wandered around the room. On a wall opposite the big painting of A Sunday on La Grande Jatte was a painting on a small piece of wood. It was similar to the famed pointillism piece but not exactly the same. The plaque next to the painting explained that this was a practice piece Seurat made as he was preparing for the bigger piece. My mind was completely blown. All my life, I had assumed the amazing artists we studied simply sat down at a canvas, and their art flowed out of them. It never occurred to me that they also had to try things out, that each piece grew from early attempts that included starts and stops and that the artist refined over time until they were ready. I think of this often now and share this with students.

Drafting is an opportunity to try different things and see what we like the most. We can choose one way and try that and see what happens. If we don't like it, we can try another way. I love the notion that it's really not that serious. It's common for writers to think that things have to come out perfectly, but drafting is about getting one version out onto paper. Drafting is about trying things out and seeing how it goes. Drafting is facing a blank page and practicing how to go from nothing to something. But, often, students need encouragement to make these first halting attempts and a safe place for approximations. In her book *Writing Down the Bones,* Natalie Goldberg (2010, 15) tells writers to say to themselves, "I am free to write the worst junk in the world." And we can too! We can write all sorts of things and it can all be junk. Or we can release judgment and it can just be. It can just be a pile of pages in our computer or desk drawer. And then when we want it to be something else, we can pull it out and look at it, sit with it, tinker with it, polish it up. I share this with students when we are collecting and drafting. This often helps them move forward when they aren't sure how to start. Reminding them that they can change it later if they want to is empowering.

No matter how a student approaches drafting, I remind them not to take the blank page too seriously. There is no failure, there is only passage of time. We try something out, and we can change it at any time. A sixth grader once said to me, "I'm going to let the storm grow in my brain, and then when I'm ready, I'll write." This is such great insight into his own writing process! He was able to articulate his needs and I was able to trust that he was in the zone even though it might not have looked like he was actively engaged in writing when I walked away.

It's common for the sixth-grade student writers to ask me how long their writing needs to be or how many paragraphs they need. I always refer them back to our checklist and that the goal is for them to be able to do everything on the checklist. Student writers in eighth grade don't ask these types of questions as much because I've worked so hard to help them know that there is no specific formula they need to follow and that length is not important. Of course, I want them to elaborate and develop their ideas but they need to decide—within their own process—how much is enough and to make decisions on what is important to include (or not).

Often in drafting, we guide students toward a specific structure in their writing. The most common example of this would be the five paragraph essay. I definitely see a value in showing students how a five paragraph essay can offer a possible structure to use to introduce a topic, give supporting reasons and evidence, and come to a conclusion. *But* a five paragraph essay, like all other graphic organizers, is a stepping stone toward future writing. It gives us a foundation from which student writers can grow and shift based on their own needs.

Releasing from formulaic writing like a five paragraph essay can be scary because we, as teachers, have less control of the final product. Teaching student writers how to look at what moves they should be able to make and then giving them space to make those moves in their own way requires us to let go of one-size-fits-all writing instruction. It might require us to adjust our thinking and, again, trust that students will find their way when we give them space to look for it. This is another invitation to a deeper connection to yourself as a writer and to your students as writers. We are exploring what writers do, which means our focus is on the thinking work we are doing when we write. Each genre brings unique moves that challenge us to bring our ideas to life. We nurture our student writers when we ask them to think about why they make the moves they make in the writing that they do. This is where we can clearly see that instead of solely focusing on the written product, instead, we are focusing on the student writers and the choices they make. When we do this, we honor the student writer and the knowledge and expertise that they bring to their writing. Centering the writer also empowers them to define for themselves what it means to live the life of a writer.

One last thought I'd like to share about drafting is that we typically look at it as part of the beginning of the writing process, but in fact, drafting can happen at any time. We can draft when we are collecting ideas. We can draft when we have chosen one idea to explore further. We can draft when we are revising. I often find that I need to rewrite or add to my writing and pausing to free write gives me a new draft to work with. Any time I'm feeling unsure of how to revise, I come back to drafting and free write something new to work with.

Living the Practice: From Free Writing to Flashdrafts

You've likely noticed that drafting involves a great deal of free writing. If you've already been practicing free writing with your students, consider showing them how extending that practice into a flashdraft can add another strategy to their writing process.

I recommend doing this focused free write in front of your students to show them how it can help them quickly develop a first draft to work with. A flashdraft is simply a free write where students write as furiously as possible across a longer period of time. This period can be a whole class period or a set time frame, say twenty-five minutes, where students focus on writing a draft as quickly as possible. Flashdrafting is different from free writing because students have more time to write and the writing should be focused on their topic and the genre they are writing. The goal is still to explore ideas but more so to develop an idea toward a draft that they can then work with going forward.

Lynda Barry's idea for how to make the page less daunting is helpful. She suggests drawing a huge X across the entire notebook page and then writing in between the X. This is a reminder to not take the page so seriously. I have also seen a suggestion to write an X halfway down the page and then challenging students to get to that X.

REVISING

It was the beginning of the school year, and we were sharing our *Where I'm From* poems with sixth-grade student writers as mentor texts for them. I shared mine and we asked kids what they noticed as we made a list in our notebooks. Then my co-teacher, Mr. Panella, shared his. As we were discussing, he explained that he had written this poem years ago when he was teaching Social Studies and then said, "I would make changes if I was going to write it now."

"You can!" I told him and we shared with the students that even though he felt like it was done years before, he could revise it.

Typically, once we have a draft that we want to move toward publication, we move to revision, but let's expand our thinking of the writing process and revision. In revision, we can make changes, start over, try something different, explore, play. Revision isn't time dependent. It isn't just one stop along the way. It threads through the entire life of a piece. Whether we are revising our idea, working with a draft, revising as we draft, or revising after we publish, revision is still available to us. Knowing this can be comforting to young writers. We don't have to get it right the first time. We'll be able to revise when it's time. It's okay to focus on ideas when drafting because revising will be there for me when I'm ready for it. When teachers talk about moving through the writing process, it can seem like writers will spend an even amount of time in each step or stage. I would say that most student writers spend the majority of time during independent writing time moving between drafting and revising. This is important to point out to student writers. If they are aware that writers move back and forth between stages and that they might spend more or less time in different phases, they can feel empowered to make the revision part of the writing process their own.

Revising is where we look closely at our writing and explore craft moves. We want to keep our mindset focused on progress over perfection and support our student writers in taking this mindset as well. The goal is to make changes in our writing to better express what we want to say and communicate with our readers. Sometimes these are small and quick. Sometimes this means trying different options, making a copy and taking everything apart, or starting completely from scratch. We'll look more at strategies to support revision in the next chapter, but know that students will likely need strategies to navigate revision and it is our job to help them see possibilities when it comes to revising. In general, help student writers see that it can be fun to explore and look at different possibilities and see which we like most.

Living the Practice: Revising with Teacher Writing

One of my favorite mini lessons to teach when it comes to revising is to look at how paragraphs help the reader. I usually do this with narrative writing, but it works in any genre of writing.

When we're studying a genre of writing, I guide student writers through the experience by modeling and offering suggestions to support their writing process. That means I'm writing with them. I brainstorm and collect ideas with them, I draft alongside them, I revise and edit with them, and I publish with them. This helps me understand what their experience is like and allows me to share my own authentic writing experience with them. I suggest you do this too.

Before looking at paragraphing, take your piece and type it up as one giant chunk of nonstop text. Display it on your large format display and ask students what they notice. Inevitably, students will notice that there is a lot of text on the screen. Ask them how it feels as readers to see all that text on the screen. Hold up a book from your classroom library that uses paragraphs and invite students to notice the difference. By now, they should be able to recognize that your piece does not have paragraphs but if not, point this out to them. Invite writers to help you think about where you can include some effective paragraph breaks. Use this as an opportunity to talk about the connection between readers and writers and also how writers use paragraphs intentionally. Facilitate a discussion about where to put the paragraph breaks and how paragraphs can show change, such as a change in setting, character, or topic. Afterward, invite students to look at how they are using paragraphs in their writing.

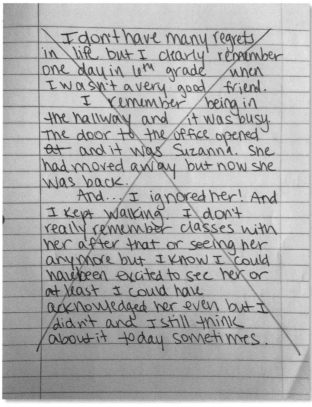

Showing Teacher Revision Process: Free Writing

Next week we'll begin dissecting our pregnant rats my science teacher Ms. Magnuson said. I cringed. Next to me, my lab partner, Derek whispered, yes. Just great, I thought to myself as I lined my books up in one neat stack on the table in front of me. I'd just rather have done anything else than dissect a smelly, dead animal. Little did I know it wasn't my lab partner or the rat that would haunt me for the rest of my life. I glanced at Derek, the chatty boy who sat next to me in Ms. Magnuson's 6th grade science class, and quickly looked away. I was never sure what to say to him and dreaded any down time. As soon as the bell rang, I hugged my arms around my books and prepared to step into the hall along with the other students of Deerpath Junior High School. A sea of 300 students stood between me and orchestra. I stepped out of the classroom and into the crowded hallway of Deerpath Junior High School.

Showing Teacher Revision Process: Typing and Shift my Focus Into the Moment

"Next week, we'll begin dissecting our pregnant rats," my science teacher said.
I cringed.
Next to me, my lab partner, Derek whispered, "Yes."
Just great, I thought to myself as I lined my books up in one neat stack on the table in front of me. I'd just rather have done anything else than dissect a smelly, dead animal.
I glanced at Derek, the chatty boy who sat next to me in Ms. Magnuson's 6th grade science class, and quickly looked away. I was never sure what to say to him and dreaded any down time. I just wanted class to be over so I could go to orchestra. *Why can't this class just be done?*
Little did I know it wasn't my lab partner or the rat that would haunt me for the rest of my life.
As soon as the bell rang, I hugged my arms around my books and stepped into the crowded hallway of Deerpath Junior High School. A sea of 300 students stood between me and orchestra. I lowered my head and dove into the sea of students, ready to make a beeline to the other side of the school. Right as I passed the front office, the door swung open and a girl stepped out of the office. Suzanna. Her face lit up when she saw me, but I looked down at my shoes and the flecks in the tile floor. I picked up my pace, nudging past other students in the hall, hoping she wasn't following me. Suddenly, I felt sick to my stomach for a different reason.

Showing Teacher Revision Process: Adding Paragraphs and Punctuation

"Next week, we'll begin dissecting our pregnant rats," my science teacher said.
I cringed.
Next to me, my lab partner, Derek whispered, "Yes."
Just great, I thought to myself as I lined my books up in one neat stack on the table in front of me. I'd just rather have done anything else than dissect a smelly, dead animal.
I glanced at Derek, the chatty boy who sat next to me in Ms. Magnuson's 6th grade science class, and quickly looked away. I was never sure what to say to him and dreaded any down time. I just wanted class to be over so I could go to orchestra. *Why can't this class just be done?*
Little did I know it wasn't my lab partner or the rat that would haunt me for the rest of my life.
As soon as the bell rang, I hugged my arms around my books and stepped into the crowded hallway of Deerpath Junior High School. A sea of 300 students stood between me and orchestra. I lowered my head and dove into the sea of students, ready to make a beeline to the other side of the school. Right as I passed the front office, the door swung open and a girl stepped out of the office. Suzanna. Her face lit up when she saw me, but I looked down at my shoes and the flecks in the tile floor. I picked up my pace, nudging past other students in the hall, hoping she wasn't following me. Suddenly, I felt sick to my stomach for a different reason.

Showing Teacher Revision Process: Highlighting Action, Dialogue, Internal Thinking, and Description

You can use your own writing to focus student attention on any element you would like to revise. Maybe you want them to look at organization, structure, leads, endings, transitions, craft moves, or how they elaborate on their ideas. Show students your writing before and after revision so they can see what changes you made and the impact of those changes. The beauty of technology is that we can go back to previous drafts if we prefer what we had before exploring revision strategies. Using your own writing as an example shows student writers you are in it with them, you are willing to be vulnerable and share your work, and you are growing as a writer as well.

EDITING

Editing is similar to revision but with a focus on conventions. I initially guide student writers to focus on their big picture ideas first and then hone in on conventions later, though, of course, we still talk about grammar choices while they are drafting or revising, and I suggest they do their best to apply these as they go. Many writers eventually find a sweet spot for editing in their writing process, and I tend to follow their needs. If we are writing about reading and a student wants to include a piece of text evidence, I take this as an opportunity to show them how to use grammar conventions to identify their text quotes. Or if we are writing narratives and students are including dialogue and internal thinking, I take a moment to show them how to differentiate by using quotation marks, commas, and tags for dialogue and italics for internal thinking. Leading mini lessons and conferring with students individually throughout the writing process gives them energy to incorporate what they have learned and motivation because this well timed instruction is empowering.

Living the Practice: Dialogue Versus Internal Thinking Versus Citing Evidence

One editing lesson I return to often is teaching student writers how to differentiate between dialogue and internal thinking and then also how to punctuate dialogue in narrative writing.

To show the difference between dialogue and internal thinking, draw a person on the board or on chart paper. Next to their head, write: I love pizza! Then, ask students what graphic novelists or cartoonists do to show a person is talking. So many students are graphic novel or comic fans that someone should be able to tell you that you need to put a speech bubble around the words. Next draw, a speech bubble around the words I love pizza! Next, write: How much longer until lunch? on the other side of the person. Ask students what a graphic novelist or a cartoonist would do to show that the person is thinking this. Someone should be able to tell you that instead of a speech bubble, you need a thought bubble. Draw a cloud-shaped thinking bubble around the words. Explain that we use a speech bubble and a thought bubble to show when a person is talking or thinking in a comic or graphic novel, just like we show the difference between dialogue and internal thinking in text.

Showing Students How Writers Make Clear When Someone is Talking in the Text by Using a Speech Bubble and When Someone is Thinking Using a Thought Bubble

Now, on your large format display, show students how to write this moment using words. Write or type: "I love pizza!" I said to my friend as my stomach grumbled. *How much longer until lunch?* I wondered. You can type it without the punctuation and italics and ask them how you can differentiate or you can show them the difference.

Pause and go back to the board, erase the exclamation mark and put it outside of the speech bubble. Then do the same with the question mark and write it outside of the thinking bubble. Ask students if that looks right for it to be outside of the speech and thinking bubbles. They should be able to see that this is wrong. Erase the exclamation point and the question mark and write them again inside their respective bubbles. Show students that just like the punctuation goes inside the bubbles, so it goes inside the quotation marks for dialogue and that it is part of the italics for internal thinking.

Making the Connection Between Punctuation Inside Speech and
Thought Bubbles and Inside Quotation Marks

When you teach citing evidence and how to directly cite evidence from a text, you can come back to this and remind students that citing evidence is similar to dialogue in that the direct quote from the text also goes inside the quotation marks—just like in dialogue.

This is one example of a grammar mini lesson that you can use when student writers are editing their work and paying close attention to grammar, mechanics, and conventions. As students reveal other editing support they need, pause to break down the meaning behind the conventions similar to how I shared here.

PUBLISHING

When we reach the end of a unit, I meet with students to decide our turn-in date. I generally have a plan for how long we are going to spend on a unit and I tell students this from the beginning. As we are working, I'll check in with them and decide if we can come to a date when they will turn work in sooner or later. Usually, about a week before, I will ask student writers to be sure to have their drafts in Google Classroom so I can check in and give feedback. I confer with them along the way but I also read over their work and leave comments for them to consider.

Once we have a due date decided, student writers work toward that. This date mainly allows me to dedicate a large chunk of time to reviewing their work all at once. When I'm ready to assess their writing, I read through everyone's pieces and make general notes about what I'm noticing. From there I grade using the checklist. Student writers are either showing that they know how to make the moves we've been working on, are starting to make the moves, or they are not yet showing evidence. I assign a grade based on this, but I also give them feedback along with an opportunity to revise based on my feedback. I know we could always keep working, but at some point, I need to assess their skills and move on.

That said, publishing should be more than turning something in for a grade. Some writing is meant for only the writer. Some writing is meant for me, an audience of one. But when I'm planning a unit, I also think about a broader audience. This brings meaning to our writing. I'll follow up with more ideas for how publishing can be folded into celebration in Chapter 6, but some examples of how we might go public with our writing at the end of a unit include reading stories aloud to another grade, performing poetry at open mics for other classes and parents, recording podcasts to share with classmates, publishing information articles in a digital publication to share with each other and parents, and presenting argument essays to administrators for them to consider our ideas.

Living the Practice: Planning to Publish

Though the publishing stage comes at the end of all this work, it actually starts at the beginning. Showing students how to begin their writing process with the end in mind is key. You can support this when you are planning a unit by giving students a direction to work toward as they begin their writing. When planning out units for the school year, show students how to hone in on a genre focus and an identified audience they'll be writing for each unit. From there, students may write a piece within that genre but the product might look different. For example, with narrative, final products could include: personal narrative, realistic fiction, fantasy, dystopian, science fiction, historical fiction, short story, or memoir. Beyond the product, encourage them to think about who the audience for their published work will be. For information, final products could include: booklets, articles, companion books, websites, brochures, documentaries, or podcasts. And, for argument, final products could include: essay, literary essay, speech, op ed, or TED talk. Finally, some final products that work for just about any genre include: poetry, graphic novel/comic, script/film.

Options for audiences might include: classmates, students from other classes or grade levels, parents, administrators, siblings, grandparents, the School Board, community members, and public officials.

Take the next unit you are teaching and identify the genre of writing student writers will be studying, what their final product will be, and who their audience will be. Share this with student writers at the beginning of the unit and discuss how keeping these things in mind as they move through the writing process will help keep them focused and productive while making their final publications even stronger. As you're ready, invite them to help you decide what the final product will be and with whom they will share it. You're helping them develop muscle memory for identifying these same things when it's time to write on their own and incorporate them into their own writing process. Letting them give you suggestions and/or be part of the decision making process can make it even more meaningful.

THE POWER OF THE PROCESS

In the end, after we have published and shared our writing, I invite student writers to reflect on their process with this particular writing piece. I recap the different mini lessons we did and match them up with different parts of the process. Then I ask students to think about the biggest challenge they faced and one thing they learned about themselves as a writer. This is important because in reviewing all that we did, student writers can see how they navigated their writing process while also reflecting on what they learned about themselves as writers.

Writer's workshop is an antidote for a racing mind. Technology gives us access to so much at our fingertips, and it's easy to jump from idea to idea, to feel the pressure to be productive, and to get things done quickly and efficiently. When I'm working with student writers, I'm always aware of what writing deadlines I have imposed upon them and which we are working toward while at the same time giving them space to write, revise, and reflect. Writing is an invitation to slow down and sit with our ideas and reflect on what we need as writers. Our writing life can take twists and turns and breaks and stumbles along the way. That is okay. We are unique and complex, we are constantly changing and evolving. We are fluid, we are mush, we are soft and malleable and here to experience joy and to keep finding ways to let joy in. After all, we are here to shine. And finding our way to a personalized writing process that works for us helps us shine even brighter.

A Moment To Reflect

- What do you think about writing as a process?
- Do you have other steps or stages you include when you think about a writing process?
- What does your writing process typically look like?
- Are there trends or common phases you move through and does it look similar or different? Where do you notice those similarities or differences?
- In what ways do you encourage your students to find their writing process?
- What adjustments might you make in your writing instruction to make room for this?

TRUSTING STUDENTS TO FIND THEIR PROCESS

In living the life of a writer we document our experiences, we explore our experiences, we share our experiences, we learn from our experiences, we savor and celebrate our experiences. Overall, it's about the writer. Everything I do as a teacher is meant to encourage and uplift student writers so they feel confident in navigating the process on their own. These learners are still at the beginning of their journeys. I want to guide them toward understanding what works for them and to feel confident in making decisions for themselves. And, though I'm required to give them grades, at least for now, I'm confident that I'm also giving them tools they can use, examples, mentors to learn from, partnerships to encourage each other, and a roadmap to support them on their path.

Earlier in our discussion, I mentioned the importance of trust. As we come to the end of this chapter, we return to this critical point. Being a writer is an exercise in trust.

Living the life of a writer means being in a relationship with trust.

Writers trust in so many ways. We show ourselves that we are trustworthy. We value telling stories and doing our best to tell them with honesty. We show up again and again for ourselves when we show up again and again to the page.

We also trust the writing process.

I define trust as 1. Competency, 2. Reliability, 3. Sincerity.

And when I think about the writing process, all three of these hold true for me. In all my years as a writer, the writing process has proven to be competent. It works. It's a real thing. It has always been that way. In that sense, it has been reliable. I know that I can do it. I know that if I move through the steps, I'll get results. I know that if I'm feeling frustrated, I can give it time, and I know it will always be there. And finally, the writing process is sincere in that it's not fluff, and it's not a gimmick. It's tried and true. It isn't always linear, but it is familiar. That said, we have to know how to wield it, and we have to make choices to help ourselves navigate it. We have to engage in the process. If we don't write, then we aren't in the writing process. If we aren't reflective, it's a very different experience to navigate. We need to put in the effort. We need to pay attention and collect ideas. We need to show up to the page and trust that the writing process works when we do. And when we experience it firsthand this way, we are learning about what it means to be a writer AS WE LIVE IT.

A Moment To Reflect

- What is your definition of trust?
- What does it look like to practice trust?
- How does trust relate to mindset and positive self-talk?
- How does trust show up for you in the writing process?

- How do we learn to trust ourselves as we live the life of a writer?
- What are some ways we trust student writers as we support them in living the life of a writer?

READY, SET, WRITE!

In writing this book, I found myself coming back to trust when I felt overwhelmed with chapter revisions. The work felt daunting. I was feeling stressed and insecure, but with my deadline approaching, I knew I had to face the work instead of avoiding it. Thankfully, I was visiting a friend, and she had to work all day which meant I had a big block of time to work and no choice but to figure out how to move forward.

Once I was settled into a spot at a nearby library, I thought to myself, *I can do this.* Then I wrote it on the page, "I CAN DO THIS!" I thought about my editor who recently had reminded me that much of the hard work had been done by drafting, so I added, "I've already done so much work of drafting." I could feel my confidence returning as I remembered to trust that writing is a process and that revisions are part of it.

As a teacher, I wish I could snap my fingers and help students move through their writing process with ease and joy. But I can't control what emotions come up for me, so why would I be able to do that for student writers?

I release control and instead, I focus on trusting that I'll navigate the emotions that come up. I focus on knowing I will find a way to move forward. I focus on trusting that there are strategies to support me if I feel stuck and friends I can reach out to. And I focus on being there for students to help them through their process as needed.

Most of all, I trust that in being a guide and giving them space to find what works for them, I am giving them the confidence to trust themselves as they live the life of a writer now but also beyond my classroom.

Writer's Affirmations

I find solace in knowing that writing is a process. In knowing and understanding that writing is a process, I focus on progress rather than perseverating on perfection. I trust that I have what it takes to find and navigate my writing process, and I know that I have access to resources to support me as needed along the way.

CHAPTER 4

Writers Know Strategies to Help Them Write

I was sitting next to Jaron while he read his personal narrative about his first away game of the soccer season.

At the time, I was an instructional coach, so I often visited classrooms to model lessons. This time, Jaron's teacher asked if I would model a writing conference for her. She was new to teaching Language Arts and openly expressed not feeling confident in knowing how to guide writers in conferences yet. She specifically wanted me to meet with Jaron because she recognized that he did a good job with factual explanations in his story but wanted to help him add more engaging descriptions.

As I listened to Jaron read, I was feeling nervous. I didn't know Jaron well, and this was the first time I was seeing his writing. Besides that, his teacher was looking to me for help. *No pressure*, I thought to myself, and went back to listening to him read.

When Jaron was done, I took a breath and said, "It sounds like you had fun on the bus ride to the game! You've done a lot of work to tell the reader all about it."

He nodded.

While Jaron wrote about the bus ride to the game, he hadn't given a description of the setting, so I decided to help him add sensory details to elaborate.

"As you were reading, I found myself trying to visualize everything you explained. Writers use our five senses to bring the story to life for our readers. If you were going to add some description based on the five senses, what would you add?"

Jaron thought for a bit. "Like how the bus smelled? And how people were talking loudly the whole ride there?"

"Exactly!" I said. "Adding details like that would help your reader."

With a specific way to elaborate on his writing, he knew which direction he wanted to go and bounded off to revise his piece.

Over the years, I've added many strategies to my writer's toolbox. If Jaron didn't take my suggestion for adding sensory details, I would have looked for another idea he might consider.

Even though I've been working with student writers for over twenty years, I still feel a tinge of worry that I won't know how to guide them during a writing conference. In general, I remind myself that a conference is merely a meeting between writers, and I don't have to have all the answers. That's not what living the life of a writer is about. I shared this with Jaron's teacher because it's important to be honest as we learn together. As teachers, we often feel like we have to be the experts in the room. It doesn't feel good to not know something, and this especially applies to writing instruction. In moments like this, I remind myself that I am a writer too, that I can relate to student writers, and that I have helpful ideas to share because of this. You can remind yourself of this as well!

We give colleagues, student writers, and ourselves a gift when we acknowledge that we are still learning and figuring things out. Living the life of a writer is about persevering through our writing process and problem solving challenges when they arise. We empower students when we show them that there are strategies available to them. Strategies that even we call on repeatedly. As writers explore their process, they also discover strategies and add them to their toolbox. This is an ongoing, lifelong endeavor.

In this chapter, I'll briefly revisit some of the strategies I've already shared, share additional strategies that you can add to your repertoire of writing strategies, and share ways to find new strategies. Even though we are learning with our students, it *is* great to have strategies we can recommend and a comforting feeling to know that we can always find resources to support us when we need them.

STRATEGIES GALORE

We're all navigating our way through our writing process and we will no doubt need to strategize along the way. A strategy is a plan of action. A strategy is simply what a writer decides to do. Being a teacher who writes means we can identify strategies that work for us and find strategies based on our own needs as writers, which we can then share with student writers. They might try on one of our strategies or adapt them to make them their own or it might spark a new idea for them. Remember, there's no right or wrong way to be a writer! There's only choices we make. And we can always go back or make a different choice next time. Celebrating progress over perfection and empowering student writers to find their own way with our support are both great lessons they can take away from living the life of a writer.

There's no way I can share all the writing strategies there are, but I can share my favorites. I'm sure you will find ways to remix these or change them up to work for you and the student writers you are working with. Take an idea and run with it! Whenever and however you are offering strategies to students, know that they are important to share with student writers so they see the ways they can improve their writing.

Let's recap the strategies we've explored so far. The first practice I shared was that writers have a way to collect. Deciding how to collect ideas is, in itself, a strategy. Strategies for collecting ideas that we reviewed included: question storming, using mentor texts as models, generating lists, making a heart map. Next, we looked at the practice of using our writer's mindset, studying strategies to flex our writer's eye including: reflecting with Lynda Barry's daily diary, writing with the five senses from a photo or camera roll, and participating in a Writer's Circle. As we explored writing as a process, we looked at strategies to navigate our writing process such as: making a web, doing stop and jots, and modeling through looking at teacher writing.

In having a way to collect, having a writer's mindset, and knowing that writing is a process, we leaned into free writing as a strategy to collect ideas, to affirm our writer's mindset, and to produce writing in different stages of our writing process.

Look at us go! These are all versatile strategies writers can use in a myriad of different ways, with different genres of writing, at different times of their process. At this point, we'll add three more equally useful and highly adaptable strategies to our collective toolbox: timelines, sketchnoting, and mentor texts.

TIMELINES

There's something about a timeline that's so simple but at the same time so robust. I can draw a line on a piece of paper, and suddenly my whole life is right in front of me on the page. I particularly love timelines for collecting personal stories to write about, but they can be used in other ways as well. Student writers can use timelines to write about a character and their experiences, to capture how a place has changed over time, and to organize a series of events chronologically but succinctly.

When kindergarten students start to take the stories they tell verbally and put them on paper, we coach them to find a beginning, middle, and end. We might ask them to tell the story on their fingers. Then we help them write across multiple pages. A timeline is an extension of this. We are inviting student writers to use a simple line on a piece of paper to represent passage of time but to expand and use this as needed to organize their ideas. This is a strategy that they can use in a myriad of different ways across genres and throughout their process.

Timelines can be helpful for identifying themes. Students can fill their timeline and then review it, intentionally looking for any themes that stand out. Timelines can also be helpful to organize scenes or moments of a longer narrative piece. This can also connect to the work we do with plot diagrams. A plot diagram, in essence, is a timeline that represents how tension builds and resolves across a narrative. While we tend to ask students to read and fill out a plot diagram after reading, sometimes their book doesn't fit into a simple plot diagram. Giving students an open-ended timeline helps them look across stories—whether they are reading and analyzing or writing them—and allows them to see how the plot rises and falls and how writers take their readers on a journey. Inviting students to use timelines while reading and writing shows the connection between being a reader and being a writer.

Timelines are also useful for gathering information writing when students are researching different sources but want to be clear about when events took place. Student writers may want to place events onto a timeline and then review the events and decide which are the most important to incorporate into their writing. They may even want to include a timeline as a text feature in their writing.

Living the Practice: Timelines

Ask students to take out their notebooks and turn them on their side. Prompt them to draw a line across the page and label it based on the timeline you want them to work with or that serves their purpose. When I'm asking students to use a timeline to mine their memories for stories, I will ask them to either label the left end of the line as 0 or as their birthday. Then ask them to label the right end of the line as their current age or as the current date. Next, ask them to add moments on the timeline depending on the purpose of using this strategy. Some options are:

- Write all the times you felt scared, successful, proud, worried, mad, sad, excited, happy. (I like making timelines for each of the different feelings to see what themes or ideas emerge.)
- Write all the memories related to _____ (this could be a person, place, or thing).
- Write all the times you learned a lesson.
- Choose a lesson or bigger theme and ask students to write all the memories related to that. For example, write about all the times related to perseverance or all the times related to the importance of trusting in yourself and others.

After students have added multiple memories to their timelines of their story, they can review them and choose one that they want to explore more. Invite them to take that one moment and to shift into free writing or flashdrafting to draft that memory.

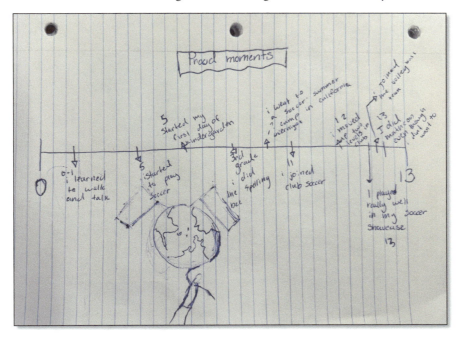

SKETCHNOTING

Just like a timeline allows writers to capture ideas visually, sketchnoting is a concrete way to represent ideas on the page as writers collect, organize, or plan ideas. I started sketchnoting in high school as a way to get my thoughts on the page and to easily represent my ideas in a way that helped me make sense of what was swirling around in my head. As an adult, I learned of the benefits of sketchnoting from educator and sketchnoter Carrie Baughcum. She says,

> When we sketchnote, we take in information with our eyes and ears, connect with the information by thinking of what parts of it are new, interesting, or make us feel something about it, then write what we've connected with in words, imagine the words, and add a doodle to it.
>
> (Vincent and Baughcum 2025)

While sketchnoting is a strategy for note taking, it's also a powerful strategy student writers can use and even a form of writing in and of itself.

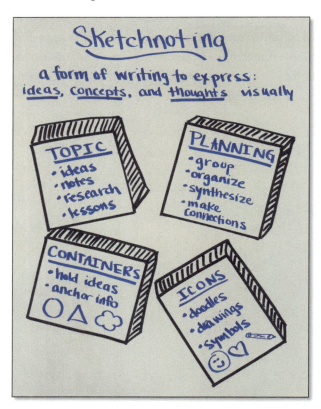

Similar to how a timeline allows student writers to think beyond traditional plot diagrams, sketchnoting gives student writers the opportunity to think beyond the traditional graphic organizers they might encounter in our classrooms. Certainly, we should introduce students to graphic organizers and encourage their use if students find them valuable. But we also want to empower students to self-select into strategies that represent their ideas in ways that make sense to them when they need it.

You'll soon find that drawing is a powerful tool for writers throughout the process. Sometimes student writers find sketchnoting helpful to unlock ideas, to organize their thinking, to plan their ideas, to identify options for revising, and even to publish. Just as a timeline allows student writers to think beyond a plot diagram, sketchnoting allows student writers to expand their thinking beyond traditional outlines and bullet points. If writing is about expressing our ideas, then making space for images, icons, and symbols to help represent our ideas is imperative.

Living the Practice: Sketchnoting

Hand out three blank notecards or sticky notes to each student. Set a timer for one minute and ask them to draw a simple sketch of a school bus. After one minute, ask students to turn and talk with an elbow partner and to tell them a memory related to a school bus. I adapted this from an exercise that Lynda Barry shares in her book *Syllabus* (Barry 2014) where she talks about the connection between images and memory. You and your students will find it amazing how drawing can bring stories to mind—but also how drawing can help writers organize their ideas. Next, give them thirty seconds and ask them to draw a school bus again. Talk to them about what elements they kept and what they were able to leave out of their sketchnote. Finally, give students fifteen seconds to draw a school bus one last time. Ask them to compare the different sketches and remind them that the point of this is to use drawing to help them write. It's not a fine art class; these sketches should be simple but meaningful to them.

Explain to students that sketchnoting is an opportunity to visually represent ideas on the page. That means we might be organizing ideas with shapes or containers, using different colors for different reasons, or using icons, symbols, or drawing to represent ideas. In essence, they are using whatever helps them get their thoughts on the page. For example, when collecting ideas for narrative writing, ask students to take out a piece of paper and draw a bird's eye view map of their neighborhood. Then ask them to label their neighborhood with different stories or memories they have there. Encourage them to use simple line drawings to represent landmarks, people, things, and even the stories that happened there. Try drawing your own neighborhood, sharing this with students as you model what this can look like. I especially like to do this after reading *My Papi Has a Motorcycle* by Isabel Quintero and illustrated by Zeke Peña (Quintero 2019). The end pages of the book show a drawing of the neighborhood and the author's note describes some of the history of the town. You may want to read the book, sketchnote the events of the story, and then invite students to create their own sketchnote to collect their own ideas. Students can then use their drawing to choose a story that they want to explore and free write about that event.

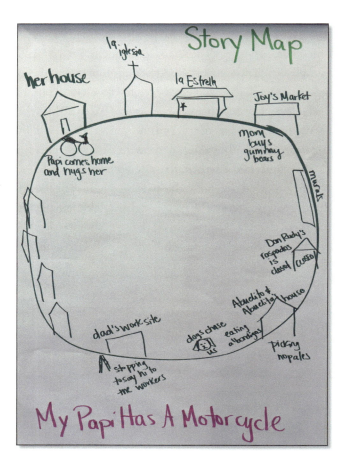

When collecting or organizing ideas for information or argument writing, ask students to gather ideas from their research. Once they have information to work with, they can use sketchnoting to organize those ideas. Show them how to look for patterns or themes in their writing. It's most common to have at least three pieces of evidence to teach about a topic or to support our claim. Ask students to draw shapes as containers and group ideas together into those containers. This is an opportunity to work beyond a single piece of paper as well. I, personally, love sticky notes, big pieces of blank paper, and my Mr. Sketch markers when it comes to doing work like this. I color code and draw lines to connect and merge ideas until I have a cohesive plan that allows me to start writing. Using sketchnoting in this way is similar to mind mapping without relying on a specific structure and incorporating words and images to represent ideas.

MENTOR TEXTS

Mentor texts are accessible, concrete, and versatile, while elevating students' writing in ways that amaze me all the time. And the coolest thing is mentor texts are all around us! From the books on our shelves to commercials on the radio to the walls or napkins or take-out bags of our favorite restaurants. Anything we read, listen to, or watch has the potential to help us as writers.

Mentor texts are any text that influences a writer's writing—as an example or non-example. I first learned of the term mentor text from Jeff Anderson in his book *Mechanically Inclined* (Anderson 2005, 16). He writes, "A mentor text is any text that can teach a writer about any aspect of a writer's craft, from sentence structure to quotation marks to 'show don't tell.'" Ralph Fletcher, when interviewed by Franki Sibberson in the Choice Literacy Podcast, explains that mentor texts are, "...any texts that you can learn from, and every writer, no matter how skilled you are or how beginning you are, encounters and reads something that can lift and inform and infuse their own writing" (Fletcher 2015). When we look closely at what other writers have done, we find moves to make in our own writing. Whether we want to replicate something or go in a different direction, mentor texts can guide us.

For example, if student writers are exploring options, they can look at multiple texts and compare and contrast choices that writers have made. They can look at leads, endings, organization, supporting evidence, formatting, text features, dialogue, description, and any other craft moves. I've found that mentor texts make writing very accessible for student writers. Essentially, you are giving them an example and a framework that they can apply to their own writing and modeling how they can replicate this same process any time they need a mentor. If student writers ever feel unsure or stuck, you can remind them of mentor texts, providing one to guide their work or helping them to find their own. I know for me, seeing what someone else has done is incredibly helpful in my writing process, so remember to model what this process looks like for students. Mentor texts are models that can be found anywhere. And, because they are concrete examples of how to make writerly moves, they can be used by any writer at any time of the writing process.

Living the Practice: Mentor Texts

Choose a text that models writing moves you want your students to be aware of, to step into, or to implement in their own writing. Display the text or excerpt. Ask the students to read it or read it aloud to them. Then ask them what they notice about the writing. Make a list of everything they notice that the writer has done—this includes what the text is about and what craft moves the writer made. After students have taken note of what the writer is doing that they would like to try, invite them to write using the mentor text as a model. Students can share and see how, even though they all were influenced by the same mentor text, they're each able to write something completely unique to themselves.

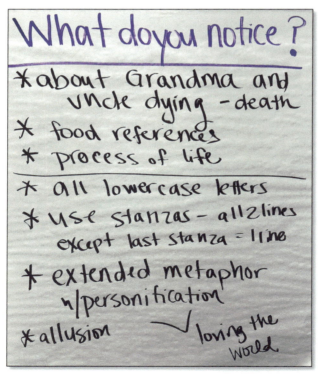

What Student Writers Noticed About Poetry After Reading
"I Loved the World So I Married It" by José Olivarez (2018)

A Moment To Reflect

Take some time to think about and make a list of strategies you personally use as a writer. Use the following questions to help you.

- What do you come back to again and again?
- Do you have strategies you use to collect?
- Do you have strategies you use to get started?
- Do you have strategies you use when you get stuck?
- Do you have strategies you use to revise?
- Do you have strategies for editing?
- Do you have strategies for sharing your work with others?

I'm an extrovert so I thrive when writing with other people. I love going on artist dates with friends to inspire my writing. I love meeting friends to write as a way to hold myself accountable. I love talking through my writing with friends to help me unlock ideas.

Make a list of strategies that you are familiar with or often share with student writers. For example, I know that adding sensory details is something I refer back to often. Similarly, I can expect to need to talk to writers about paragraphing and how to use paragraphs to signal a change to a reader, so I have a strategy I use to help them with that. Think through different stages in the writing process and also different elements of writing that you might have strategies for.

After you have a list of strategies, think about what resources you might use to share these with students. For example, could you do a simple notebook entry modeling each of the strategies? Or could you create an anchor chart to put up in your physical learning space or your digital learning space? When conferring with writers, you never know what strategy might be great to share in the moment, so having an awareness of what strategies you can share and an easy way to share them will help you feel confident during writing conferences.

STRATEGIZING ABOUT STRATEGIES

Strategies are available to us at any stage of the writing process. Whether we are collecting, planning, drafting, revising, or editing, there are strategies we might use naturally and strategies we can enlist when we aren't sure how to move forward. Remember that strategies help us move through our writing process but each writer can decide their own plan of action.

In Chapter 3, I mentioned standards and checklists I co-create with students. I use these to guide student writers and will often use these as a third point that we can refer to. For example, if a student tells me they are done or if they ask me if I think they are done, I say, "Did you look over the checklist?" Depending on the student, if they say they haven't, I'll either sit with them and go through it or send them off to review it on their own. Oftentimes, as we look at their piece together and go through the checklist, they'll find something to revise. Using standards, rubrics, and checklists helps us narrow in on how we need to guide our writers and what strategies might be helpful to them.

Strategizing with the end in mind will help us identify strategies that might be helpful to student writers. For example, I know that eighth-grade students need to be able to convey a theme or lesson in their memoir writing, so I can make a plan to have strategies ready to help them be able to do this. I can offer an exercise to collect story ideas based on a theme or lesson or I can share a mentor text that can prompt them to think about themes.

As students move from collecting to drafting, some students will take their ideas and be ready to write. Still, others might benefit from a strategy to plan or organize their ideas a bit before going off to draft. A great way to make space for these different approaches is to release students who are ready to go off and write. Those who might need a little more direction can stay and meet to discuss options. Or you can share options and then let students decide whether they are ready to write or whether they need to plan a bit more.

Planning strategies could look like filling out a plot diagram for narrative writing or outlining for information or argument. I will often model during whole class instruction or have samples to share with students as needed so they can see how planning can be helpful. Sometimes it's as simple as writing three bullet points on a sticky note and drafting from there. Just remember that we are offering strategies to support student writers, not to control their writing process. The goal is for them to understand themselves better as writers. This means they can recognize what they need and make a decision or we can offer options to support them as needed. Providing a menu of options or ideas for student writers to consider goes a long way in helping them see what possibilities are out there.

Sixth-grade student writer, Carla, asked me to meet with her to discuss her Where I'm From poem. I could see how she had structured her writing but she hadn't visibly organized her piece into stanzas yet. All her lines were on the page one right after the other. We looked at the mentor texts we had been studying and I asked her what lines she would group together into stanzas. She moved some lines around and split them up so she could see her stanzas more clearly. Once she could see the stanzas, I asked her what she noticed about them. She could easily see that one stanza only had one line.

"That might be an opportunity to write more," I told her.

"But what do I write?" she asked. This question showed me that she needed guidance in how to do this. Having a strategy for a situation like this wasn't in her repertoire yet.

I offered some options for how she could expand and talk more about that part of her life or add a description like she had in her previous stanzas and she nodded and got to work.

Being a writer myself has helped me add a lot of strategies into my repertoire but I still plan for conferring with student writers by anticipating what strategies might be useful to have accessible to share. If I'm not sure, I do some research. Books like Jennifer Serravallo's *The Writing Strategies Book* (2017) are a great resource but I've also learned to be comfortable with telling students that we need to find a strategic way forward together or to ask the class for suggestions. Remember that we're all living the life of a writer and that means we're all figuring out what that looks like. We don't have to have all the answers.

SHARING STRATEGIES WITH STUDENTS IN CONFERENCES

Other than mini lessons, conferring with students is where I find myself sharing strategies the most. Time to meet individually with writers is absolutely essential to my instruction because it allows me to differentiate and support students through their writing process. My whole class instruction during mini lessons gives students broader grade level support as they navigate working toward a published piece. But, small group work and 1:1 conferences allow me to make suggestions based on what I'm noticing when I look at students' individual writing and as I assess their writing needs in the moment.

Over the years, I have found that having a plan for when I'll confer with student writers and making a schedule helps me. During independent work time, I'm either pulling a small group of student writers or meeting with student writers 1:1. I'll ask if anyone needs me to check in with them but I also keep a list to make sure that I meet with everyone. If I have a co-teacher in the room, we have a shared list so we can make sure to connect with every student writer.

I like to keep records of who I'm meeting with, when I meet with them, and what we discuss. This helps me notice trends, observe student writers' progress, and think about what strategies I need to have ready to share. I generally begin conferences with a few basic questions:

- What are you working on?
- How's it going?
- How can I help?
- What are your next steps?

For me, simple is best and, with these questions, I focus the conversation I'm having with the student writer. Most of the time, they'll share what they are working on and naturally tell me what they're grappling with, or I'll paraphrase what they have said and acknowledge the work they are doing. Then we talk more about it, and I'll ask questions or offer new strategies or remind them of strategies they have in their toolbox that might help. Before I leave the conference, I always ask them to tell me what their next steps are. This gives them a chance to recap what we discussed and make a strategic plan for themselves. Oftentimes, they'll write this down for themselves on a sticky note.

Conferring with student writers lets me learn more about their thinking and how they are navigating their process. As they share their work and ideas, I also get feedback on how my mini lessons are going. I can see how student writers are applying the strategies I've shared and how they are making them their own. Though it may take some time and finesse to get it right, I can confidently say that conferring makes an impact. Start with one student. Keep it simple. Take it slow. But make it happen.

A Moment To Reflect

How do you feel about conferring with student writers? Explore the emotions that come up when you think about meeting with individual writers. As you sit with the emotions that come up, ask yourself what would help you address that emotion. If you have positive emotions, that's great! Let's capitalize on those. Brainstorm ways you can lean into what is working. If you have negative emotions, that's totally okay too. Brainstorm what you might do to help yourself reduce some of the negative emotions.

Living the Practice: Launching Writing Conferences

Once you have your writer's workshop and its routines established, announce to students that you will be starting individual writing conferences. Explain that these are opportunities for you to connect with each student individually to hear how their living the life of a writer is going and to offer individualized strategies for them to consider adding to their writing repertoire. Display your note-taking method or what questions you are using to guide your discussions and go over them with students. You may want to invite a student to help you model what a writing conference might look like. Invite students to ask questions about the process.

When you are done, tell students that their work as writers is to be engaged in living the life of a writer while you confer with students. Tell them that you are going to meet with a student writer and give them your attention. Ask students what it should look and sound like while you are doing this. Make a list on chart paper so students have an understanding of what they should be doing while you are conferring. You can even brainstorm what they should do if they need something or encounter a problem. Leave these up on the board while you release students to start working. Give students a few minutes to settle in before sitting down to confer with your first student writer.

I recommend pausing after that first writing conference to check in with the whole class. Point out what they did well, and let them know how you felt while conducting the conference. Then ask them if they have questions or if anything came up that they need help with. Remember that monitoring student behavior and checking in with them is ongoing and the more structure you give students, the more they will be able to feel confident to engage in the work independently.

ADDING MORE STRATEGIES TO YOUR REPERTOIRE

I love meeting with student writers and other writers in general because I get to hear their strategies for living the life of a writer. Thanks to technology, there are so many ways to learn from other writers. Looking online, you'll find people have shared insight into their writing life in so many ways. Whether it's something they have published personally on their website or blog, or something that has been shared about them like an article, an interview, or a video, there are many ways you can see into a writer's life. Show your writers that they can do this as well to build on their own strategies.

For instance, if you aren't sure how to help a student, you can invite them to do some research and see what they find. Maybe hearing how their favorite author finds ideas or what their favorite author does if they feel stuck can give a student writer a way forward with their own writing.

The awesome librarian at my school works with me to bring authors and illustrators in to meet with students. When we're preparing for a guest visit, I make sure students think of questions to ask related to the author or illustrator's process. I also pay close attention to the writing strategies these authors and illustrators share during their presentations that I can point out to students after the visit. By doing this, we are making an explicit connection between the writing students are doing and the writing that published authors and illustrators are doing. This affirms students' identities as writers. It also helps them see that the strategies we are using in our classroom are similar to the ones that writers use beyond school.

Living the Practice: Researching What Our Faves Do

Either individually or in whole or small groups, lead a search about a favorite writer and either their writing advice, or their writing process—for example, Jason Reynolds's brainstorming ideas or Elizabeth Acevedo's writing advice. Show students how to explore the search results while looking for ideas to try, and then try one together. Remind students that learning strategies from professional writers is about finding what works for them. They'll want to think about what might work and what might not work for them. Also remind students that whether a strategy works for us or not, we can still add it to our repertoire, because we never know when it will come in handy at another time in our writing lives.

A Moment To Reflect

Pause to make a list of five writers whose writing you enjoy. Do a little personal research on each of them. You can start with their websites and then do a deeper search about their writing process.

- What do you notice about the strategies you encounter?
- Is there something that they do that resonates with you?
- Do you see any strategies that you already use or share with students?
- How does it feel to learn from published authors that you admire?
- Did you discover any new ideas that you'd like to try?

READY, SET, WRITE!

Overall, our goal as teachers is to give students tools or strategies they can use to be independent. While I value the writing communities and partnerships I'm part of, I ultimately know that my writing falls to me. I preface my feedback to student writers by reminding them that I am just one person with thoughts to share. I have knowledge and expertise that I know matters, but I also honor the writer and the knowledge and expertise that they bring to their work. My goal in centering the writer is to empower learners to understand what it means to live the life of a writer and help them define what that means themselves, using all the strategies available to them.

As educators, giving students options and empowering them to make their own choices is important for engaging student writers in discovering their writing process. Instead of being told there is one way to write regardless of whether that way works for them or not, students are invited into living the life of a writer in a way that resonates with their writer's heart. This requires that we shift from telling students our way of navigating the writing process and instead invite them to explore the myriad of different strategies with us.

Ultimately, we are all on a continuous journey of living the life of a writer. Our students will continue to learn and try and evaluate and grow writing strategies as they move through their education and beyond. By sharing other writers' processes with them (including our own!) and showing them how to discover more strategies for themselves, we set them up to confidently navigate their writing process in a way that works for them no matter what they are writing.

Writer's Affirmations

Instead of feeling stuck, I strategize, knowing that there are strategies available to me when I need them. I can learn from other writers, whether I know them personally or through my research. I have strategies in my toolbox or the ability to add strategies to my toolbox that will help continue to grow my understanding of what living the life of a writer looks like for me as I navigate my writing process.

CHAPTER 5

Writers Explore

Eighth-grade student writers were spread out around the room and their quiet voices filled the air. They were meeting in pairs to study our mentor text, an excerpt from Sy Montgomery's memoir *How to Be a Good Creature* (2018), through the lens of structure. Together, we had read and annotated the chapter about her encounter with an octopus named Octavia. Then I sent them off to reread and explore the writing from the standpoint of a writer gathering clues for how to write their own memoirs.

As students flipped through the pages and marked up the margins and took notes in their notebooks, I circulated the room, listening in. Here and there, I asked questions or guided them, but for the most part, I gave them space to grapple with analyzing a mentor text in this way.

Afterward, I brought all the students back together and asked them to share what they had noticed. In sharing their ideas, we were able to consider what was similar and what was different but also explore connections between what we noticed as readers and what a writer does to weave together stories and information to reveal a bigger message.

Memoir   Memoirists examine mentor texts through a lens of structure

- Writer tells a story, teaches, goes to a memory moment, shares a tough question - different order
- Writer gives background information
- Mood changes based on what she is dealing with
- Writer deals with questions in her head - internal thinking
- Writer uses sections - divides the story up
- Writer includes action, reveals about character, some suspense, teaching, to reveal a final message - each section but overall as well
- Has a problem that writer works through to reveal an aha moment
- Writer includes compare and contrast
- Writer takes time to teach their knowledge - shares research
- Writer connects the ideas to help the reader
- Writers starts paragraphs in different ways - transitions, facts, dialogue

---

Our group of writers was able to see that Montgomery moved between storytelling and teaching. We were able to see how she works through a problem while sharing the questions she's asking in her head until she reaches an aha moment. They were also able to see writing moves like including action, giving background information, using transitions, sharing facts/research, and incorporating dialogue.

Before this lesson, we had started collecting big life lessons students might want to explore in their memoirs and looking for patterns to support them. After studying Montgomery's text for structure, I invited them to choose a moment in their life and to start writing in an effort to tease out its bigger life lesson or meaning.

I encouraged students to flashdraft so they have some writing to work with. This is an extension of our free writing practice (mentioned on page 20) that invites them to write long but (hopefully) uninhibited. As we have already seen, free writing is a journey in exploring, in sitting down to see what comes out when you face a blank page. This free writing was focused on a topic with the intention of developing a bigger theme, while remaining open-ended. Going forward, I encouraged their writing, met with student writers in writing conferences, and coordinated meetings with writing partners—all the while, keeping the essence of exploration at the forefront of our writing work.

This brings us to the focus of this chapter: writers explore. Living the life of a writer means being curious and open to discovering how to persevere through the writing process. We explore the world, we explore ideas, we explore how we navigate the process and the mindset it requires to do so. We explore what other writers have done, strategies that might support us, and ways to honor the work we are doing.

In writing, I truly believe that there is no right answer. There is only a drive to stay curious and try things out. Writers explore by taking on a mindset of *what if* and we can support student writers by encouraging this and making space to model and talk about what this looks like.

We've already looked at how to notice ideas all around us and to harness positive affirmations. We also established that writing is a process and made space for students to discover their autonomy in what their process looks like. And, we've unlocked the power of strategies and how to identify even more strategies to help us when needed. The essence of exploration is present in all of these. Living the life of a writer means constantly being open and trying new or different things.

So, in this chapter, we'll look at how growing a community of writers who regularly share what living the life of a writer looks like empowers all students with their exploration mindset. We'll also revisit the reader–writer connection and the importance of nurturing a community of readers in a writing classroom.

A Moment To Reflect

There's a certain nudge for control that comes with being a teacher that, when managed intentionally, results in a loose-tight structure that allows space for our instructional guidance but makes room for individual writer's needs. Though we can co-create our space and develop a classroom community with our student writers, at the end of the day, we have to make decisions and design lessons and guide our students forward toward the instructional standards they're held to. In the end, we are the ones whose job it is to work toward those outcomes. That means exerting some necessary levels of control in our classrooms.

Exploration requires that we release some of that control to allow for and encourage students to choose different pathways to reach the same end result. Enter, once again, trust. To give up control means to trust student writers to be curious and to take risks and to reflect with us. Let's pause now to think about your personal connection to this truth.

- How do you feel about exploration?
- What emotions do you feel in your body when you think about giving student writers more space to explore?
- Do the feelings have a positive or negative connotation or both?
- Are there any underlying fears you can recognize?

AN ATTITUDE OF EXPLORATION

My grandfather was a groundskeeper and when I think of the shed that was his workshop, with tools and parts and supplies everywhere, the words "neat" and "orderly" do not come to mind. I'm sure it was organized to him, but there were things all over the place, tucked here and there, hanging from the walls. He would tinker with things and get things to work. To some, his space might have looked like chaos, but he gathered bits and pieces that he might need and he was willing to put in effort to explore how to get things to run smoothly.

Living the life of a writer is about more than believing in yourself as a writer. It's also about knowing how to persevere mentally by embracing a writer's mindset of openness, curiosity, and willingness to explore. In order to help students persevere through the writing process, we have to cultivate an attitude of exploration. We've worked on our writer's mindset, we have gathered strategies, and we understand that we move through our writing process. Now, like my grandfather, it's time to put effort into exploring.

Explorers understand that they can develop their skills and that there are strategies available to them. Explorers are open to putting in effort, learning from their experiences, working through obstacles or roadblocks, responding to feedback, following others' lead but also forging their own way. Explorers are okay with discomfort and learn how to navigate it. That's what it means to persevere through the writing process.

It's important to recognize that we, as educators, are guiding our students, but they are the writers. Yes, we are the ones assigning a grade in the end. Yes, we have specific learning targets for them to meet. Yes, this is our job. But we must remember that they are the writers. They are the ones adding words to their pages, rearranging, making decisions, deleting. Our job is to teach them the attitude they need to show up to the blank page and to work through their writing process.

We understand that our student writers are doing creative work within an educational system that was designed for students to be compliant, to conform to expectations, and to march through the curriculum. Our awareness of this helps us anticipate what student writers might need and how we might address them. Just as there are so many ways to live the life of a writer, there are a variety of options for persevering through the writing process. It might look messy or unproductive, but that's how writing is sometimes.

We need to be conscious of how we view productivity and how we nudge students forward. Over the years, I've adjusted how I approach workshop and how I guide student writers, and it all goes back to my relationship with control. The more I write myself, the more understanding I have. There are times when I need to stare into space and let my brain sit with an idea. There are times when I need to look up a word and go down an etymology rabbit hole so I can feel confident in how I use a word. There are times when I need to watch an episode of *Friends* to be able to make a reference to it. There are times when I need to give myself a break and go for a walk to clear my head. There are times when I need to break out my Mr. Sketch markers, stand in front of some chart paper, and dump out all my ideas. Do all of these look super productive? Probably not. But do they all count as living the life of a writer? Yes. They do.

Writers try on all sorts of strategies to find what helps them navigate their process. Knowing that these strategies have worked for me helps me recognize that student writers also need space to explore their process. I structure my class as a workshop so that student writers have space to figure out how to work through their process. It might feel a bit scary at times, but I trust that the more I step back and release my semblance of control, the more opportunities I am giving to my student writers to grow confidence in themselves. Teacher writers hold space for student writers as they navigate toward their independence.

After my mini lesson, I release student writers to work. Before I do, I will often make a list of options for what their next steps *might* be. I do my best to focus our mini lessons so students find value in them, but I don't expect every single one of them to immediately apply the ideas from the mini lesson in their writing. The work from our mini lesson is definitely one option but we'll explore others together. Sometimes I encourage them to settle on their focus because this requires them to make a decision and leave with a focus in mind. They can then move around the room, sit with others, take bathroom breaks, use the supplies in the room, and use their time as they decide. During this time, I move around the room and confer with students. Of course, I make sure to maintain an environment where everyone can work, but this work can look different for every student writer if needed. In my conferences, I will often give students a few options to choose from. Especially if a student writer isn't sure of how to proceed or wary of how to move forward, I like to give them options and then step away. I'm never forcing my ideas onto a student writer. I might know exactly how I would proceed but I don't assume that the student writer will or presume that they need to do things my way. I'll offer options and then let them sit with those ideas. Sometimes a student knows their way forward but has trouble articulating it, so stepping away to give them space to explore their next steps is important.

The positive affirmations we identified when discussing a writer's mindset in Chapter 2 can come in handy here, but guiding students toward actions they might take can also help them. Our goal is to help students expand their thinking so that they understand they have choices and then allow them space to explore and choose for themselves.

A Moment To Reflect

Think about what thoughts or feelings come up when you think about a student staring into space during work time. Sit with that and write about it.

- What thoughts or feelings emerge?
- Can you identify where these thoughts or feelings come from?
- What do you need to know or hear in order to help yourself give students space to reflect as they explore?

Living the Practice: Supportive Check Ins

When we ask student writers to reflect on their writing process and share with each other, we bring their attention and awareness to the ways in which they navigate the writing process but also remind them that there are different pathways for doing so. In this way, we show them that they have options and can explore what it looks like to live their personal navigation of the writing process. To do this, you can lead supportive discussions, before, during, and after independent work time.

Before Independent Writing

After your mini lesson, before you release students to work, ask them to share what work they will be engaging in during the independent work time. I will often make a bulleted list that students can refer back to during their independent work time.

On chart paper or your large format display, write the words, "You might…". Then ask students to share what their next steps are. Phrasing it in this way gives student writers choice while also opening them up to different ways forward with their writing. In hearing what others share, they might stick to their plan or try something different but you've given them the opportunity to explore and contributed to their mindset of not having to do things one specific way.

> # You Might...
>
> — take 5 minutes to breathe
> — reread our mentor text
>   to look more closely at :
>   • theme
>   ◦ form /structure
>   • style /craft
> — gather ideas from your notebook
> — list ideas
> — free write/ draft
> — brainstorm with a writing partner
> — check in with Mrs. Vincent

During Independent Writing

Another way you can facilitate conversations like this is during independent work time. When conferring, make sure to conclude your time together by asking the student writer what they are going to do next. This allows them to reflect on the discussion and also to decide for themselves what they want to do next.

As you confer with students, remember that they are resources to each other. If you are conferring with a student writer and it reminds you of a conversation you recently had with another, invite that student writer into the conversation. Pause the conference and tell the student writer that another student writer had a similar situation. Ask if it's okay to ask that other student writer to share what they did. Invite the writer in to share what they experienced and how they were able to navigate it. Let the student you are conferring with ask any questions. Thank the visiting writer for sharing their experience. Make connections between the different writers' experiences and ask if the student might want to try what the other writer did. They might be open to trying what the other writer did, or perhaps listening to what they did might spark a new way forward for them. Our goal is to be a guide and encourage them but ultimately, writers need to be free to explore options and make their own decisions.

After Independent Writing

After independent work time, when it's time to reconnect and share, you can invite students to share what they did, what options they considered, and what their process across all of this looked like. Similar to charting this before they go off to write, start a list of what students did do. In a T-chart write or type, "Options we explored:" and then invite student writers to share what they tried under the second column, "Choices we made." Explain to students that sometimes they are doing similar work as their peers and sometimes they are making individualized choices based on what they need and that it's okay if these look different.

ANTICIPATING STUCK SCENARIOS

Hiro Hamada, the main character in Disney's *Big Hero 6* (Hall and Williams 2014), needs to invent a project to get into an esteemed tech school that his older brother attends. At first, he's excited and motivated, but soon he's at a standstill. He's shown literally holding his beautifully sharpened pencil above his paper and not being able to write anything. He then gets mad at himself for having no ideas. His brother playfully scoops him up and holds him upside down, telling him not to give up but, rather, to look at things from a different perspective. This is where a writer's mindset meets exploration. Sometimes, we have to shake ourselves out of our inertia and start to explore the task through varying perspectives.

Just like we accumulate strategies to help us move through our writing process, so do we need to learn strategies for when we might feel stuck. We have acknowledged that we all move through the writing process in our own way. Now, it's important to acknowledge that feeling stuck and knowing what to do if we ever feel stuck can also be unique to every writer.

Over the years, I've learned that I love finding ideas and I love drafting. For me, it feels very freeing. Revision, on the other hand, feels like work and I notice that I tend to avoid it rather than run to it. Because I know this about myself, I've explored strategies to help myself when this happens. We can bring our students' awareness to this by facilitating discussions about what feeling stuck might feel like as well as what to do if we ever feel stuck.

Sometimes, like Hiro's brother suggests to him, we need to take a different angle. The great thing about writing in community is that student writers have access to their peers and to us. Together, we can help them see opportunities that they might not be able to recognize for themselves. If a student expresses to me that they aren't sure how to move forward, I'll ask some questions and then offer ideas. I tend to give two or three ideas so that they are able to see that they have options and that there isn't only one answer. Additionally, I make sure to let them know that they might come up with another idea. Sometimes, a student will take my idea, and then my job is to encourage them. And other times, a student will want to think or will come up with their own idea, and then my job, again, is to encourage them. Feeling stuck, after all, is often an opportunity to grow confidence. Whatever move they decide to move forward, we can champion their progress.

Living the Practice: Navigating Stuck Scenarios

Show the clip from the Disney movie *Big Hero 6*, mentioned earlier, where Hiro is brainstorming his project for the tech school. After the clip is over, ask your student writers what Hiro did when he got stuck. Guide them to the advice Hiro's brother gave him to look at things from a different angle. Ask student writers if they have ever felt stuck while writing. Explain to them that writers know that the writing process won't always go smoothly. Sometimes it will, but not always. Invite student writers to turn and talk about what advice they would give to someone who feels stuck like Hiro does before his brother gives him advice. Bring writers back together to share their ideas. Record the ideas on chart paper. You can keep this posted in the room for future reference and for students to add to over time as more ideas come. They may want to keep a personalized list just like it in their writer's notebooks. Remind them that writers explore and something they might explore is things they might try when they feel stuck. Writers, after all, have a mindset of exploring and finding ways to persevere through the process.

To take this one step further, put students in pairs and ask them to come up with a scenario where a writer is stuck. Then have them share ideas that the writer could try or explore.

Another option would be to post different scenarios and place them around the room on chart paper. Students can do a carousel and walk around the room, leaving advice for the writer on the chart paper. This could be added to their ongoing collection of ideas for what to do if they ever feel stuck and need to explore ways to move forward.

WRITERS SUPPORTING WRITERS

As you're growing a community of writers, explore ways student writers might support each other. Sometimes this happens naturally—a student writer asks another writer to read their work, a student asks for help, someone laments about what to do next and another writer gives them advice. This is amazing when it happens, but we can also teach students how to explore options and ideas by conferring with each other and give them an opportunity to try this out.

After we have been working on our first writing piece of the year for a while and students have solid drafts, I match them up with a writing partner. When I'm setting up writing partners at the beginning of the year, I review student writing (either their on-demand pre-assessment or the pieces they are working on). Then I match students with writing partners who are showing similar strengths. For example, I might pair the two student writers who scored the highest on the on-demand pre-assessment and then continue to match partners similarly for the whole class. Or I might match the student writer with the highest score with a student writer who scored in the middle of the group, and then continue to match down from there for mixed ability pairs. You'll find the right fit for you and your students, but I've found that matching student writers with a partner who is similar in ability generally makes for richer and more balanced conversations. Once students have the experience of working with a writing partner, they can meet with a writing partner at any time, though I also continue to schedule time for them to meet with assigned or self-selected writing partners throughout the school year.

Over the years, I've noticed that students take their work as writing partners seriously and this pushes their thinking about what writers do. Their discussions mirror what we discuss and practice together in mini lessons, the language we use to talk about moves writers make, the checklist and rubrics we use to guide our writing, and comments from my writing conferences with them too.

I often open a student writer's document to discover comments that a writing partner has left for them. Sometimes they drop in editing advice or spelling notes. Sometimes they leave constructive feedback for the writer to consider. Here's an example of an eighth-grade student writer's comments for her writing partner:

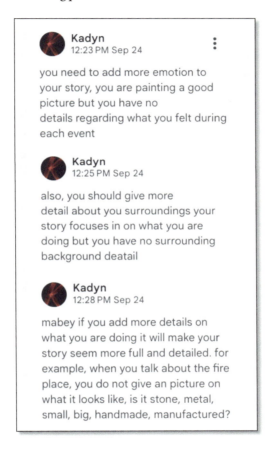

In this instance, the student is inviting her writing partner to add internal thinking and add description to the action he already has. She even uses the word "mabey" to show that she isn't positioning herself as the expert. But she does have examples to support her suggestion so that her partner can recognize what she needs as a reader.

Seeing student writers meeting with each other, whether I've helped to facilitate their meetings or not, warms my writing teacher's heart. They are exploring what writers do when they read a peer's writing. But they are also opening their eyes to what is possible when they apply what they know about living the life of a writer to supporting their peers. Writing partners is just one example of growing a community of writers and fostering their exploration while doing so.

Living the Practice: Peer Coaching Conferences

Think about the conferring system you use regularly with students. Then model so your students can replicate this in partnerships. In my classroom, I make a similar version of the Google Form I use for conferring and add in a space for the student coach to record their name. If they need a bit of a scaffold, I sometimes give writers choices for how to respond to their coach's feedback. Certainly this isn't as open-ended as when I'm leading the conference with a student writer, but it largely mimics that process. I find that this scaffold helps the coach take notes while also helping the student writer focus their answers. They take turns asking each other questions from the form and then will read each other's writing or listen as their partner reads their own writing and then discuss. You can decide how you want to match partners based on what you think will be the most helpful for the writers you work with. Then explain how they'll work through the conference with each other, modeling and scaffolding as needed, and give them time to meet with each other.

READER AND WRITER CONNECTION

Developing a community of readers is part and parcel when fostering a community of writers. And exploring this connection when living the life of a writer is imperative. There are so many resources for how to nurture students as readers. The more we encourage students to explore texts through their readers' lenses, the more understanding they have of how stories flow and how ideas fit together. As we've learned previously, absolutely anything can be a mentor text. Even inviting students to think about other content they consume opens them up to thinking about how ideas are shared.

In this chapter's opening example, we used the excerpt from Sy Montgomery as an anchor text for memoir writing, but I also invited students to choose a memoir to read independently during the unit. We then looked for similarities between everyone's selected memoirs and explored the variety of moves writers made in those texts that students could try in their own memoir writing.

I'm also lucky to work with an amazing librarian who helps coordinate author visits with our local independent bookstore. When we welcomed author and illustrator Ruth Chan to our school at the beginning of our memoir unit, I prompted students to pay attention to what she shared about her memoir writing process and to ask questions about her methods. After her visit, I referred back to these ideas, using them to guide students forward with their research for their own memoir writing.

While this book focuses on helping student writers explore what it means to live the life of a writer, it is also imperative that we help students see the connection between consuming and creating. For example, if a student enjoys reading a certain genre of book or enjoys a specific medium, it's important that we honor that preference while also inviting them to explore how that might influence their own writing.

Reading and writing go hand in hand. I remind my students again and again that there are literally people in the world who study how to help students become better readers. And do you know what they have found? That the students who read more are better readers. Obviously, as educators, we know there is more that goes into helping student readers grow but exposing them to books and other reading media as well as lots of opportunities to read texts that interest them is critical.

When we study mentor texts, I invite students to look at what the writer did and then try writing something with their own twist. I'll always remember my student, Raven, and her tendency to write pieces that were gory or creepy. These are exactly the books she gravitated toward. She read *Sadie* by Courtney Summers and *Monday's Not Coming* by Tiffany D. Jackson. It wasn't a surprise, then, that she would write something gruesome and yet intriguing when given the opportunity.

Similarly, Edith is a voracious reader of realistic fiction and it makes sense that she tends to write with very honest, internal thinking and bringing out ideas that reflect the kinds you'd generally find in the realistic fiction that she reads. Themes like sibling rivalry and family matters are common in her writing.

Students want to share their stories. They will rise up with incredible results when given the space to explore and feel appreciated for their efforts. Just like giving students time to read is critical, so is giving students the opportunity to write. Encouraging students to live the life of a writer means giving them plenty of opportunities to face a blank page, exploring what ideas come forth along with new ways to navigate their writing process. The more students face a blank page with our guidance, the more willing they will be to explore a blank page independently in the future. And if not willingly, then at least I hope I've helped them face a blank page with less trepidation.

Living the Practice: Book Talking Mentor Texts

To encourage students' independent reading habits, invite them to share book talks with each other. I've done this in a variety of ways over the years but I always go back to what I call the original, or OG, Book Talk. The OG Book Talk involves a student standing up in front of the class with their book and talking about it. Start by thinking about the most recent book you've read that might speak to your students. Write up a brief summary of the book. You can keep it simple by going back to the tried and true summary template of: somebody wanted, but...so then. Decide how you might get students interested in the book without giving away the ending. Be sure to share what type of reader you would recommend this to. For example, you might recommend a book to someone who likes suspense or enjoys Dystopian books. Finally, share what writing moves you noticed the author using or ideas you might take into your own writing after reading the book. Present this to the class—you can wing it, practice it, or read it directly from a script.

Then, ask students to prepare their own OG Book Talk based off of your model to present to the class. This works best if they share a book they recently finished or are currently reading. Decide when your students will share their book talks with each other. This could be a student every day to start or end class, or a handful to share on Fridays. However you decide to make time for it, know that students sharing their favorites with each other is a powerful way to grow a community of readers and writers.

READY, SET, WRITE!

Living the life of a writer means exploring what we need along the journey. In this chapter, we revisited this as part of the writer's mindset and acknowledged that writers are always exploring—whether it's gathering ideas or refining their process or collecting strategies to enhance their writing or just getting unstuck when they're feeling unsure, stuck, or blocked. We looked at ideas for how to shift into curiosity and to make space for exploration as we live the life of a writer within a community of writers and readers.

Exploring options together is such a great experience because, in doing so, we create safe spaces for students to see that there is no right or wrong way to navigate their writing process. In this way, we reaffirm the idea that writing is a process while also inviting them to discover new strategies that might work for them. As a community living the life of writers, we can come together and share ideas like this with one another, while considering what this might look like at different stages of their writing process. Giving student writers the opportunity to share their process and to pick up strategies from others is powerful.

In truth, we've only scratched the surface of what writers can explore. Here are some additional opportunities that you might want to consider:

- personal mentors,
- finding support,
- favorite genres,
- craft moves,

- mentor authors,
- supportive peers,
- what type of feedback works,
- what writing environment works,
- what conferring setting/format works.

Living the life of a writer can be a journey into the unknown. Embracing exploration means trusting that we will find our way forward and guiding our students in this mindset as well. Embracing exploration means releasing control of the process and the path and the product with tons of freedom to meander, to start and stop, to feel a full range of emotions, and to persevere through it. While exploration runs through each practice we discuss in this book, it's crucial to remember that embracing exploration is ultimately about giving students practice in how to stay curious every step of the way.

Writer's Affirmations

There are endless opportunities to explore in every aspect of living the life of a writer. Whether I am exploring how to expand my writer's mindset, strategies to help me navigate my writing process, or ways to celebrate my progress, I approach living the life of a writer with curiosity and an open heart.

CHAPTER 6

Writers Celebrate

Our poetry writing unit was coming to an end, and Rogelio asked for a writing conference, so I could give him feedback. During our conference, I showed him places where I was curious about what was going through his head in the moment. He did a wonderful job bringing a small moment to life in his poem, but I didn't yet see where he was sharing his internal thinking in order to contribute to the deeper meaning of the piece. We started the unit by watching Phil Kaye perform his poem "Before the Internet" (Kaye 2018), brainstorming meaningful moments in our lives, and thinking about lessons we learned from those experiences. From there, we looked at common poetry moves to bring a moment to life in order to share that bigger lesson with the reader.

During our conference, Rogelio said, "This is fun."

"Yeah, it is. It's kind of like solving a problem or putting a puzzle together," I told him.

Sometimes student writers think getting feedback means they will need to rewrite their piece. And while this can sometimes be the case, more often than not, there are ways to use what they have by reorganizing, adding, or developing what is already there. While writing and living the life of a writer doesn't take one exact shape or form, there are still some common ways we can look at our writing objectively and bring forth meaning.

More commonly, student writers want to turn in their writing, get a grade, and be done with it. But conversations we have with student writers should empower them to embrace the productive struggle. Living the life of a writer is a lifestyle. It's not about getting the grade, it's about having a story worth telling and the devotion to telling it well.

When we left our conference, Rogelio seemed to hear what I had to say—both the naming effects of his writing and the areas where he could strengthen what he was trying to convey—so I was excited to see what he did with the feedback I had given him.

The next day, I called out to him over the hustle and bustle of eighth graders making their way into class.

"Yes?" he answered, placing his things on the table in front of him.

"I read over your revisions."

"Oh, yeah?"

"Yes! And I have to tell you that the changes you made brought tears to my eyes!" I explained.

He shrugged and said, "I didn't change that much."

"I know but the internal thinking you added throughout made such a difference. You showed your vulnerabilities and it took the entire piece to another level."

"Thanks," he said.

To Rogelio, his changes didn't seem that significant, but to me, they were worth celebrating. I made sure to point out how impactful his revisions were as soon as I saw him because I was proud of him for how he elevated his writing. He took his writing to another level because he was open to feedback, willing to sit with it, and eventually made thoughtful revisions. Much about living the life of a writer is worth celebrating if only we pause to recognize our efforts and take the time to celebrate. This chapter is dedicated to just that—making time to honor and appreciate all that living the life of a writer entails.

From the beginning of this book, we have been celebrating, and you've likely noticed this thread of celebrations moving through all the previous chapters. When we personalize our notebooks, we are celebrating our unique and complex identities. We are saying, "Look at me. I'm a writer." That is worth celebrating. When we notice things all around us and capture them in our notebooks, we are celebrating life. Whether what we are capturing makes us happy or sad, angry or surprised, or any other type of emotion, when we write it down, we are acknowledging and honoring the truth and that is worth celebrating. When we show up to the page and move through our writing process, that is worth celebrating. When we share our writing with others, be it a teacher or a writing group or partner, we share our progress, welcome feedback, and show our commitment to growth, and that is worth celebrating. When we polish up our writing, publish it, and share it, that is worth celebrating.

At the start of this book, we celebrated our lives as writers by identifying a way to collect our ideas. We made this personal and celebrated stepping into identifying ourselves as writers. Next we celebrated our writer's mindset—recognizing our efforts to find stories all around us as well as to affirm our writing practices. We explored our writing process and strategies to support us through our process. We celebrated our progress and our efforts to learn about what works for us and ways to move forward with awareness of what works for us. Finally, we looked at exploration and celebrated a mindset for inquiry and asking *what if*.

Student Writers Celebrating Their Personalized Notebooks

Now, we'll center celebration as an integral practice of living the life of a writer. In this chapter, I'll share the importance of a mindset of celebration, what constitutes celebration, and how we can embed celebrations throughout the writing process and throughout our time with student writers. Cue the confetti! Let's celebrate!

A MINDSET OF CELEBRATION

We all have different experiences and different ways that we show up in the world. Maybe celebrating is easy for you, but I know that as a teacher, it's much easier to celebrate my students than it is to celebrate myself. At the same time, I also know that sometimes I get so caught up in how my students can grow and how I can help them work toward a published piece of writing that I have to remind myself to celebrate with them. I've learned that I need to be intentional about celebration for myself and for my student writers.

Not only do I practice being intentional about celebration in general, but I'm also mindful of celebrating throughout the process. Celebration is often positioned at the end of a writer's process when it's time to publish, but I assert that writers should celebrate often and throughout the writing process—and throughout their writing life. If I only celebrated when I published a book, then I would rarely celebrate, so I'd like to invite you to also think beyond publication when it comes to celebration. Our student writers write a lot and designing opportunities for them to share their writing with others is important, but publishing shouldn't be the only time we celebrate. The process should be celebrated along with the product. That means thinking about all aspects of living the life of a writer and finding ways to celebrate throughout.

Just like we can foster positivity and practice exploring, so can we nurture a mindset of celebration. Celebration is a mindset. When we open our eyes and our hearts to recognizing what can be celebrated in our lives as writers, we notice more and more all that we have to celebrate.

Start from a mindset of celebration when working with student writers. Instead of looking at what student writers cannot do (yet), approach student writing to first see what they *can* do. With this attention, dedication, and focus to celebration, we help our student writers experience joy in living the life of a writer and give them an example of what this can look and feel like.

As we nurture our mindset of celebration, let's remember that celebration falls on a spectrum. Celebration can be as simple as pausing to smile at yourself for what you have accomplished—big or small. Or it can be as elaborate as a culminating publishing event. We have made space for variety in each of the practices so far and celebration deserves the same. After the work we have done in this chapter, hopefully you have ideas for how to celebrate and, in turn, see your student writers in a way that resonates with them.

A Moment To Reflect

We can find opportunities to celebrate throughout all aspects of living the life of a writer. Be on the lookout for opportunities to show your students how you do this in your own writing. When I'm drafting, I often check in on my word count because adding words to the page is how I can see I've made progress. When I'm revising, I am more likely to keep track of time I have spent revising as a way to celebrate my progress. Bringing my experience as a writer into my classroom has helped me make space for student writers and their process.

Think about ways that you celebrate your writing progress. Close your eyes and remember the feeling that comes with those celebrations. Make a list of different ways you like to celebrate and that feel meaningful to you. Star the ones that you could easily replicate in your classroom. Draw an arrow next to the celebrations that you might be able to modify and model for your student writers.

WHAT CONSTITUTES A CELEBRATION?

As we've already discussed, living the life of a writer is a personal experience. It makes sense that our ways to celebrate can also be personal. When I first designed my free writing habit loop, having a phrase that acknowledged and honored me as a writer was helpful to me as a celebration. Over the years, I've realized that being an extrovert also greatly impacts what living the life of a writer looks like for me. I thrive off of talking with others as a way to brainstorm, as a way to move through problems, but also as a way to celebrate. Sometimes I need to text a friend to ask them to celebrate with me. I'd love to support student writers in developing their intrinsic motivation, but I'm aware that external motivation can play a part in celebration too. Before we go further, let's get curious about what constitutes celebration.

If every writer is unique and every writer finds their own unique way to live the life of a writer, then celebration can be equally unique. We might each have a different vision of what is worthy of celebration. We might each have a different idea of what counts as a celebration. Similarly, we might require celebration to support us differently. I've worked with student writers who don't want a lot of fanfare. And I've worked with student writers whose faces light up when I point out what they're doing well in their writing. In truth, it might not be as flashy or extravagant but instead, meaningful.

As you get to know student writers, I'm sure you'll get a sense of how to celebrate each of them. But it's also a great idea to ask them to think about what type of celebrations resonate with them. This might be something they can articulate easily or it might be something they need to think about or experiment with.

Here are some examples of ways you and your student writers might celebrate:

- affirmations,
- high fives,
- sharing with a friend,
- getting a positive compliment from a friend,
- sharing work somewhere,
- sharing with the class,
- dance party,
- cheer,
- stickers, stars, or stamps,
- checking off a box,
- choosing a new pen/marker,
- taking a break,
- calculating how many words are written,
- logging minutes spent,
- tracking progress toward a goal,
- getting a treat or prize (like a piece of candy or a laptop sticker),
- checking in with someone,
- looking back over a piece and giving yourself a pat on the back.

Inviting student writers to think about and explore ways they prefer to celebrate gives them ownership for affirming their writing identities. Their celebrations might be something you can join in on, like giving them a big smile or a high five when they share something to celebrate. Or their celebrations might be something you need to remind them to do for themselves personally or amongst each other. Helping young writers see that celebration can take many forms and supporting them as they infuse celebration into their writing lives is important.

A Moment To Reflect

Before sharing with students, take time to think about how you define celebration.

- What does celebration mean to you?
- What do you consider to be a celebration of yourself as a writer?
- What are some ways you typically celebrate your writing life?
- What are some ways you would like to try celebrating your writing life?

Living the Practice: How do *you* Celebrate?

Ask students to think about times in their lives when they've felt seen and appreciated for something they did or accomplished. Share some of your own examples as a model and then let them chat with a partner about ways they celebrate something they are proud of. Maybe they can think of ways they celebrate when they have been part of a sports team or how their family celebrates birthdays or other important events. Invite pairs to share and add to their lists.

Once you have a list generated, talk to students about intrinsic and extrinsic rewards. Go through the list and mark each type of celebration with an I for intrinsic and an E for extrinsic. Discuss the benefits of both. Discuss how it's our own intrinsic opinion that really matters, though extrinsic recognition might be motivating. Next, create a new chart and ask students to think about how some of these celebrations might be applied to their writing lives. If a volleyball player loves the cheers their team does after an ace serve, maybe they can come up with a writing cheer. If a student writer loves when their family gets together for birthdays or other events, maybe they can help plan a class celebration or invite their family to celebrate their writing. Bringing awareness to the variety of ways people celebrate and applying that to our lives as writers is a way to excite student writers about their writing life but also a way to affirm their work in a personal way.

To take this a step further, ask student writers to think about where these types of celebrations might fit into their writing process. Are there some celebrations that can span their entire writing process? Are there certain celebrations that feel more specific at certain stages during their writing process? Maybe they can recognize some simpler ways to celebrate and some more significant ways to celebrate and start to match both to different parts of their process. It might even be helpful for them to plan future moments for celebration so they can look forward to those celebrations throughout their writing process.

CELEBRATE WITH OTHERS

Enid walked over and held her computer up to me. "I think I'm done," she explained. "Will you tell me if this is good?"

I've realized that some students come to me when they want validation that they are done or that their work is good. In this request, I can see that she is seeking my approval and also looking for validation of her work, so I turn the questions back to her.

"Did you look over the checklist?"

She nodded.

"Okay, so is there anything you still want to work on or do you feel confident in what you've written?"

Sometimes the student writer is just ready to be done. Other times, they know there is still something to work on. That's what happened with Enid this time.

"Well, I'm not sure about the ending. What does it mean by giving insight for the reader to consider."

This is an invitation for a conversation. We can look at her work and decide together whether she is able to show that skill. Once I sense she feels confident, I ask her how she feels and acknowledge her efforts. I'm happy to celebrate her, but I want to make sure she develops her ability to see herself and what it feels like to have a sense of pride in herself. My job is to be aware that when she first approached me, she was seeking a celebration and then to coach her.

Because I know Enid, I have grown to understand how I can celebrate her in a way that also empowers her. Just like I have grown to understand Pete. When he's written something, he gets excited and will call me over to read it because he loves it.

"Read it. Just read it," he'll often say, but his request comes more from a place of already thinking what he's written is great and wanting to share it with me.

When I'm done, I'll point out what I notice or what stands out to me. And then I'll ask him if he wants feedback or if he's good to keep writing on his own. There's a difference between informally talking to student writers about their writing and conferring with them. In a conference, the understanding is that we're actively working on their writing together. During workshop time, our interactions don't always have to be as deep as conferring conversations, although sometimes they are.

Nurturing conversations like this might be the most simple and most natural way that we can celebrate in and out of a classroom. The idea is to simply tell someone what you have to celebrate. It's important to acknowledge the work you are doing but it's easy to tell someone else and invite them to celebrate with you. Because we are lucky enough to be in community with other writers in a classroom setting, this is a great way to celebrate. This can look like students coming to you to tell them something they achieved (or vice versa), but it can also be a turn and talk to an elbow partner at some point during class, a check in with a writing partner, or the end-of-class share. Creating a culture of celebration means inviting students to share their wins and to celebrate them again and again. We've already talked about how writers can support each other through hard times, but this is a way we can support each other through the good times too.

Bring your awareness to how you respond to students when they share writing updates with you. Of course, smile, give them a high five, give them a compliment, but recognize the opportunity to celebrate even if it might not seem like they are asking you to celebrate. You most likely do this naturally already but it's worth bringing our awareness to it so we can make sure that we do help students celebrate. Sometimes we move along, when pausing to give a student writer a few extra seconds of our attention will go a long way.

While we want to encourage our students to be able to independently live the life of a writer, that doesn't mean they need to be completely isolated as a writer. Connecting with other writers who can empathize with our experiences is important. When we celebrate with each other in a classroom, we show student writers what it looks like to be in community with other writers and others, in general, who support them. Developing this mindset shows student writers that we can be inspired by each other and lift each other up rather than feel envious or competitive in an unhealthy way.

STATUS OF THE WRITING CLASS

However we choose to celebrate, we first must pause long enough to recognize and acknowledge our efforts or our progress. With a class full of student writers and a limited amount of time that we're with them, every minute counts. That's why I like to take a quick status of the class related to our writing. I don't do this every day but I will do it more often when further into a unit and students are in different places with their writing.

You may be familiar with status of the class as a way to check in with students on their independent reading. I first learned of this from Donalyn Miller in her book *The Book Whisperer* (2009). There are different ways to apply the strategy to your writing class.

I typically create and display a slide with a grid and add each student writer's name to its own box. Before releasing students for independent work time, I ask them what they plan to work on and type it into the box. This works for a few reasons: it invites each student to take ownership of how they are going to spend their time, it shows how we are all committed to our writing while honoring that we all move through the process in our own way and in our own time, and it allows me to celebrate them where they are. If Suho is working on getting a first draft out, I might give him a quick thumbs up and let him dive in. If Aleksa is adding dialogue after a mini lesson, I might give her a nod and tell her it's a great idea. With practice, this can happen quickly while still being meaningful.

Earlier, I mentioned ending with an invitation for students to share. That's a celebration! Sometimes, I take my status of the class at the end of writing time instead of or in addition to asking students to share. At the end of independent writing time means students have a chance to check in with themselves and to acknowledge how they spent their time. You can even do a double status of the class—at the beginning and again at the end.

Taking a status of the class in this way is an easy way to acknowledge student progress and offer support as needed. By doing a quick check in like this, student writers bring their awareness to their process, give us insight into their process, and celebrate. Not to mention, making the time for this sends a clear message that checking in with ourselves and pausing to celebrate is important.

USING CHECKLISTS TO CHECK IN

Students were working on argument essays, but I noticed that Curtis wasn't engaging in the work. After asking him about it, he said, "It's going to take forever."

I had printed the argument writing checklist for all students, and he had it out on the table in front of him. I sat down next to him and pointed at the checklist. "Let's take it one step at a time. I'll talk you through it."

We started with the claim. He was able to verbally tell me his claim, so I immediately said, "There you go! Write that down!"

Once he had typed it into his document, I again pointed to the checklist. "Okay, guess what? Now…" I dragged out the word before exclaiming, "you get to check. the. box!"

The look he gave me was one of exasperation, but when I handed him my favorite green felt tip pen, he took it and checked off the box. We continued to work through the checklist with my excitement growing every time he was able to check off another box. It took time to sit with him and willingness to be a little cheesy, but it worked. He made great progress on his essay and soon he was checking off the box without my prompting.

Never underestimate the feeling that comes with checking a box! I've been known to make a list just so I can cross things off my list. It is a seemingly small but mighty celebration.

Similar to matching a strategy with writing needs, so too is it important to match our enthusiasm and our celebration with our student writers' needs.

I mentioned earlier that I use checklists for students to develop their writing. I also use criteria for success to help them check in with themselves on a daily basis. While taking a status of the class allows me to take a quick pulse of where students are, checking in offers some structure and guidance for students as a benchmark for their progress. Here's an example of where living the life of a writer outside of a classroom might be different from in the classroom. School provides a structure when it comes to time. There are classes and semesters and school years. There is also an expectation that we are assessing student writers' skills. At some point, I need students to submit work for me to evaluate compared to grade level standards.

Based on the time I have allowed for a unit of writing, I guide student writers by giving them benchmarks and check-ins along the way. At the beginning of a unit, student writers know what checklist I'll be using to apply a grade to their writing as well as how they'll be sharing their work. This checklist becomes a resource for them. My mini lessons guide them, but they use their independent writing time to move through their own process at their own pace.

On a daily basis they always have the overall checklist, but I also check in on them compared to the time we have and we discuss a general idea of where they should be. With discussion, students become confident in their own process. For example, one time Landry heard me share that most students should be in a place of making final edits and he didn't feel that he was that far along. After asking some questions and talking about his progress, he realized he was closer than he initially thought to being on target to turn in his piece. While I strive to give my students space, the nature of school means they have to adjust to meet a deadline and/or navigate the consequences of not turning in a done piece. There's a balance between nurturing them as creatives and adhering to systemic expectations. Again, I find that conversations and reflecting together helps us navigate this together.

You might recognize this as an executive functioning skill, and it is. Process writing is the act of taking a final product and breaking it down into smaller tasks and then taking action to get it done. In a writer's workshop, we're coaching writers to take action and learn what works for them while also gaining an understanding of how long things take and the broader skill of accomplishing a long-term project. My dad used to tell me, "Anything is possible if broken down into manageable segments, stabilized by balance, and purified by belief." Making this connection for student writers can help them understand how powerful a checklist can be for them in writing and in other areas of their lives.

As student writers share their progress with me, I'm intentional about asking some follow-up questions here and there, offering ideas, and of course, acknowledging and celebrating their progress. This might feel very similar to taking a status of your class, but know that some students will appreciate the structure and a concrete plan that comes with having a checklist for what to work on and how to move forward as well as someone who checks in on their progress. And, like Curtis, they might love celebrating by checking off a box.

LEVERAGING A GRATITUDE LIST (AKA WHAT'S WORKING)

Much of living the life of a writer is about momentum. If our job as teachers is to inspire student writers to write, to sit down at a blank page and make something out of nothing, then we need to be aware of how to do that and how to pass that along to our students. Fostering an attitude of gratitude is a powerful gift we can give student writers. We've already looked at a writer's mindset to celebrate stories all around us and to affirm our writing identity. Now, we look at how we can practice gratitude as part of our writer's mindset.

Being grateful for what you have experienced and what you have learned is powerful when living the life of a writer because there are so many ways to live the life of a writer. We can be grateful for identifying what works and what doesn't. We can be grateful for having strategies that work now and strategies that might work at some point in our lives as writers.

Practicing the shift from complaining and feeling stuck to instead noticing what is working or what has worked before will help you bring some positive energy to your student writers.

Ask students to write about what they are grateful for when it comes to living the life of a writer. Depending on your students, you might coach them to zoom in or to zoom out. Sometimes zooming in is helpful because students can see exactly what they are doing and the importance of it. Sometimes zooming out is helpful because it gives them a broader context for what it means to be a writer.

It might be something like being grateful for spell check or speech to text. Or it might be something like being grateful for the opportunity to have time and space to write.

You can make a list together or ask students to work independently.

When I confer with students, I usually ask them what is going well. This essentially is asking them what's working. I take notes on this so I can remind them when we need something to celebrate that is going well. Sometimes this helps them unlock a path forward. For example, if someone is stuck, I might remind them of something they did in the past and invite them to bring that into what they are working on now. We can be grateful for what's working and celebrate it by acknowledging it in the moment or at a later time.

TREAT YOUR WRITERLY SELF

I wholeheartedly believe that teaching writing should be joyful. We're talking about ways to celebrate in this chapter and sometimes, celebrating means rewarding yourself for the work you've put in. Pausing to acknowledge, affirming your process, sharing your progress, checking off a box are all worthy celebrations. If you and your student writers find that you need to step it up a little bit, think about treating your writerly selves.

When I talked about habit loops in Chapter 2, I pointed out that a behavior is reinforced by a reward, or something positive to look forward to. In our free writing habit loop, pausing to read or say the affirmation is the reward. Some other rewards might be doing a little dance, taking a stretch break, or chatting with a friend. I wish I could say that my motivation for writing is completely intrinsic but the truth is, extrinsic motivators also come into play.

In 2019, my first year teaching in a classroom setting, I worked with a group of students who were in seventh grade and in a sheltered English as a Second Language class for Language Arts and Social Studies. Two of the students were newcomers to the United States but the others were born and raised in the United States, speaking Spanish as their native language. One student in particular was very disillusioned with school and his anger impacted the whole class. I was familiar with gamification but had never tried it with students before. As a tech coach, I had gamified professional development (PD) for teachers I worked with and then supported a teacher who wanted to gamify her classroom after the experience she had in the PD. Thinking of how to connect with this student and the class, gamification seemed like it could bring some novelty to my classroom.

With the support and encouragement of my friend Carrie Baughum, I brainstormed and designed the first game I would use in my classroom. At the time, I was focused more on behavior. Students chose a character for their Mario Kart and earned the opportunity to roll a dice and move along a Rainbow Road that ran around the room. Since then, I have shifted to design a whole unit where students complete quests (writing about reading and writing in response to reading picture books), and after completing a quest, they check in with me to go over their work to receive Book Bucks. I've become more comfortable with knowing how to gamify. It requires some creativity and a willingness to take a risk, but I've found that when done in a purposeful way, it is completely worth it.

While I don't gamify every unit in my classroom, I do recognize that it's motivating to student writers when I do. There are other ways to reward student writers—like tossing them a piece of candy for offering an idea or putting a stamp on their paper or in their notebook or giving them a laptop sticker after a furious flash drafting session. I tend to offer rewards like this sporadically and to make it a surprise. It's important that you consider what feels right to you and what your student writers would benefit from.

Spontaneity can be fun, but there's also something to be said for predictability. You can invite student writers to design a chart so they can track their progress toward a goal and identify how they'll reward themselves for meeting their goal. Some student writers benefit from a clear plan and a defined reward. If they can focus on writing for twenty minutes, then they can take a walk. If they write every day, then they can choose a prize on Friday. Again, remember to check in with students and allow them to give you input on what would feel celebratory to them while also making sure it aligns with your values and your budget.

ADVENTURES IN WRITING

I work to be a responsive teacher who adapts to the needs of her students. That means I adjust my teaching depending on what students need. Sometimes I adjust my mini lessons based on what students need to learn but other times, I adjust my lesson plans based on what students need emotionally. Writing requires mental energy. Sometimes we need to go on a writing adventure. By that, I mean taking a mini break for an unusual and exciting writing experience.

In my experience, students enjoy getting to play games in class. I've collected word-related games that I keep in my room for when we need a bit of a brain break. Even though it's a break, we're still thinking about words and stories. Some of my favorites are Tapple, 5 Second Rule, Scattergories. Don't assume students know how to play the games. I often highlight a game or two and show students how to play, or play the game as a whole class to give students an idea of what fun is in store for them.

I especially love taking a day to pause our usual class structure to play a writing-related whole class game. Three of my favorites are: Disruptus, Grudgeball, and Spare Change Game Show. Disruptus is a board game from FoxMind that I bought and modified to help students come up with an idea and describe it to others (FoxMind n.d.). There's an opportunity to compete with others and use some argument writing skills if you'd like. Grudgeball is a game I learned from Kara Wilkins at her blog To Engage Them All (Wilkins 2013). It's a highly engaging review game that I use to practice grammar skills we have practiced in class. Each team has thirty to sixty seconds to write a sentence using a specific grammar skill. Grudgeball is a game that students beg me to play but I reserve it for an end-of-the-quarter celebration (Wilkins 2013). And finally, the Spare Change Game Show is an activity I discovered from Amanda Cardenas at Mud and Ink Teaching (Cardenas 2024). In teams, students flip a coin to find out whether they need to debate the pros or cons of a topic. This is a great way to put argument writing skills into action in a fast-paced, fun, collaborative way.

Share with students how proud you are of how they have been working and let them know that you've decided to take a little pause to play a game. In this way, these games are a reward and therefore a celebration, but also still meaningful toward the writing they've been engaged in.

REFLECT TO HONOR YOUR PAST, PRESENT, AND FUTURE

Reflection is a powerful part of living the life of a writer. As important as it is, we often only think about it as looking back. But reflection is, in fact, a two-part process. First, a writer does need to look back and be honest with themselves about how things are going. Second, they then need to use that honest reflection to inform their future decisions. Reflection is an act of looking back in order to move forward. Sometimes, we reflect on an experience and realize what we need to continue our efforts or amplify them. Other times, we reflect on an experience and consider what needs to be eliminated or changed. Or, often, there's a mix of behaviors to keep and something to shift.

When we invite students to reflect, we give them ownership of their effort and agency to choose a path forward. I'm always impressed by how reflective student writers can be when I build these opportunities into my lessons. Though sometimes unconscious, students are often aware of what is or isn't working in their writing or process. Asking them to share whether it's verbally or in writing helps bring that awareness to the forefront. In doing this, we are, once again, putting trust in the student writer and nurturing that trust in themselves to know what needs to change or what needs to continue.

Reflection isn't a flashy celebration. It's subtle and can easily go unnoticed, but reflection truly is a celebration of the effort a writer has been putting forth. Reflection is not about dismissing what has been done, instead, it is about acknowledging while also adjusting if necessary.

Teaching literacy is teaching humanity. As educators, we understand that being a reader and being a writer means paying attention to what it means to be human. We read to understand how humans move through life—both internally and externally. We write to share how we move through life—both internally and externally.

In middle school, there is a shift in the depth of what students are expected to write. Students go from sharing their stories and opinions to being expected to write in order to comment on a social issue or to share a point of view and to use evidence from their lives and from their research to support the argument they are making.

This requires student writers to reflect on their experiences and to be able to articulate their thinking. Reflection is an integral part of being a writer. If we don't reflect, we run the risk of prioritizing productivity. Yes, writers write. But living the life of a writer should include celebration so that we include time to reflect and honor the work we are doing. Pushing to add words to the page or pushing to publish without taking time to celebrate could result in burning out or not finding joy in the journey. We're already so hard on ourselves, we have to be wary of being hard on ourselves as we are living the life of a writer.

One way we reflect on our lives as writers is during the writing process when we confer with student writers or when they confer with each other. I also make time for them to reflect at the end of every writing unit. I display the writing process on the board and together, we review and list all that we have done. I ask students to think back to the work they did collecting ideas, studying mentor texts, making plans, using strategies, drafting, revising, editing, and publishing. I ask them to think about what went well, what was difficult, what they learned, and what they might do differently next time. I give students time to write in response to prompts to reflect and then we share.

When we are reflecting in the middle of a unit, I often ask them to share how things are going and offer a prompt for them to respond to. Sometimes they give me great insight into how I can be helpful and other times, they reveal that they just need more time to keep working. Either way, bringing our attention to their progress and their process is beneficial.

Reflection invites students to think metacognitively about their writing process. With a class or classes of student writers, it's not always easy to know what students are thinking or what is resonating with them. While reflection is important for students, I also find it valuable to me as a teacher. They celebrate themselves when they reflect but I celebrate our work together when I read their reflections. And then I use that information to guide my mini lessons and conferences going forward.

For our student writers, it's imperative that we model how to take time to reflect. I know how precious time is. I know the pressure of making every minute count and getting to everything the curriculum requires of us. I'm guilty of feeling like we need to keep moving forward and wanting to rush things, so I have to remind myself to take the time to reflect and to give student writers time to reflect. Practicing reflection as a celebration grounds us in the present. In an on-demand world with technology demanding our attention, slowing down to be present might not come easily, but it's still important. Reflection is also a valuable life skill in general. It might take a little more time, but it's worthwhile. Trust me.

Living the Practice: Writing Prompts for Reflection as Celebration

For this activity, you can decide to pause where you are in your writing unit or wait until the end. On your large format display or chart paper, review what student writers have done, creating a bulleted list as you do so. Choose a few of the following questions and ask students to write a short answer response to these questions.

1. What small or large parts of this unit can you celebrate?
2. What line or section do you love to silently reread to yourself?
3. What challenges can you celebrate overcoming?
4. What can you celebrate about yourself as a writer?
5. What is something you might continue to do or do differently next time?

A NOD TO PUBLISHING PARTIES

In most elementary classrooms, publishing parties are scheduled for the end of a writing unit as a way to celebrate. But this type of celebration tends to occur less and less frequently as student writers progress through middle school and high school.

While I encourage you and your student writers to explore different ways to celebrate, thinking about a culminating celebration, such as a publishing party, is still worthwhile.

I, personally, think that having a plan to share writing with an authentic audience is important. When I'm ready to launch a new unit, I think about the final product students will be creating and who they'll be sharing it with to ensure student writers have opportunities to share their writing with others in and out of our classroom. Our sixth graders have shared their personal narratives with the fifth graders in a fall storytelling event we call Story Society. In the spring, sixth–eighth graders have shared a writing project of their choice at a showcase that we invited fourth and fifth graders, as well as families, to attend. We have held an Open Mic where students share poems with their classmates, with third–fifth-grade students, and then for families at an evening event. Seventh and eighth graders have had a reading day at the end of our memoir unit where they had time in class to read and respond to others' final pieces. Eighth graders have shared their TED Talks about success after reading the book *Outliers* by Malcom Gladwell (2008). And sixth graders have written investigative journalism articles that we published as a digital magazine.

These are just some examples of what publishing and sharing with an authentic audience can look like. These are opportunities for student writers to have a wider audience beyond only me, their teacher. I suggest considering ways your student writers can share their writing with multiple audiences—both in and outside of the classroom. Consider asking your students how they would like to celebrate their hard work and with whom they would like to share their writing. They will most likely have great ideas and will feel more motivated, since it was their idea.

A Moment To Reflect

Take time to review your scope and sequence for the year. Make a list of the writing student writers engage in during your class. Consider where you might layer in celebratory moments along the way. Ask yourself what celebration looks like at the end of a writing unit. Are students turning writing in to you? Are they sharing with each other? Are they sharing with a wider audience?

After you notice, ask yourself if there are ways to invite student writers to have input on how they celebrate their process as well as how their published pieces are shared and celebrated. You might brainstorm some ideas for how they can connect with an authentic audience and then ask for students to weigh in and be part of the planning for how to celebrate.

A CELEBRATION OF SPACE

"Are we picking seats today?" Keon asks as soon as he sets foot into my classroom. It's Friday, and we choose flexible seating for the upcoming week on Fridays.

I smile, "Yes, we're choosing seats today."

He's not the only student who notices rhythms and routines. Others will ask about things they look forward to or come to expect when they walk into my classroom.

Keon reminds me of myself when I was little and my birthday would come around. I was always eager for people to arrive and for the party to get started, and at some point, I couldn't help but ask my mom when I would get to open presents. (In my family, we opened presents after cake; I knew this, but I would always ask anyway.) Keon knows what's coming and is anticipating it. Maybe it's not as exciting as opening birthday presents, but the tradition feels like celebration.

We should consider the space and structure of our classrooms a celebration. I hope that students feel celebrated when they step into my classroom. Their work is on the walls and materials are accessible. In fact, most everything is for student use. Students have a variety of flexible seating to choose from—we have large tables with traditional seats, tall tables with stools, a couch, beanbags, a mini couch with a small table, and two seats with another small table. A student is assigned to lead the seat-picking for the week, and we have very clear expectations for how flexible seating is used, but they love the option to move to choice seating. The space contributes to the work we do as writers.

Similarly, there is something to be said about the structure of the class and how it contributes to our efforts as writers. In general, we have a common routine that we follow in writer's workshop. Whether it's a daily routine or a weekly routine, this structure offers a predictability that can be seen as a celebration. Knowing that it's coming gives student writers something to look forward to.

There's also something to be said about a routine as a sort of tradition. We're here, and writing is what we do. I often take off my rings and put lotion on my hands as a signal to my brain that it's time to write. The repetition of this over time has made it feel like an act of respect every time I do it. I'm honoring myself every time I show up and repeat this routine. It brings me into a focused state as I say to myself: *Here I am. I am a writer. It is time to write.*

In my classroom, Keon isn't the only student who loves knowing what his flexible seating will be for the week. When students go off to write, they love to go to their spot and settle in. It isn't only special seating though. Having a structure for the class overall, having an attention getter, using sounds in class like a chime, a doorbell, playing music, having a specific saying or catchphrase, having materials available, asking students to take out their notebooks—all of these done in a repeated way comes to feel a celebration. The message to student writers is: *Here we are. We are writers. It is time to write.*

READY, SET, WRITE!

I'd like to invite you to zoom out a bit with me. Yes, we have a limited amount of time with our student writers and very specific standards and expectations we need to meet and address with them. It's easy to get caught up in what we need to get done, but if we zoom out, we can see that we are giving young people the time, space, skills, and confidence to write about their lives and lived experiences. We are giving them an opportunity to show that they matter by sharing what matters to them.

There's a reason the most common type of graffiti is someone writing their name or initials or writing, "I was here." By asking students to write, we are showing them that their stories are worth telling. That, in essence, is showing them that they are worthy. Writing, in and of itself, is a celebration. Because don't we all want to know that we matter?

Getting to write with young people is a gift in and of itself. I repeatedly remind myself of this. Yes, teaching has its challenges, but we get to work with young people, and they're amazing. Let us remember to marvel at the humans in front of us, honor their lived experience, and appreciate the ways they show up in the world. This is cause for celebration!

We admire writers for being able to capture a moment with words. Not only do they write in such a way that we feel like we were there or are there again, but we feel the gravity of the moment. They bring the moment to life but also the emotions that were being felt. We love the writers who can make us feel. To feel is to remember that we are alive. In a world where technology makes it so easy to detach and numb our senses, writing invites us to connect to our humanity and to sit with our senses.

Remember that as teachers, we are creating space for student writers to explore what it means to live the life of a writer. While we are working toward standards and skills, it is also our responsibility to care for the student writers in front of us. In inviting students to live the life of a writer, we are inviting them to be writers for the rest of their lives. Whether they actively pursue publication or write just for them in the future, developing their identity as writers deserves a celebration. Writing is empowering and we get to help them realize this. You elevate the student writers in front of you by celebrating them and their efforts in living the life of a writer.

I think life is amazing, and I bring that sense of awe into my life as a teacher. I'm forever impressed by what students do in my classroom. When I think about the effort they put into their learning and how I can nurture that, it comes down to giving them access to what I'm asking them to do as much as celebrating them and their progress.

Writing this chapter took a lot of introspection for me to be able to articulate what celebration looks like in my classroom. It's so intricately woven into everything I do that it's subtle and almost imperceptible. I imagine you might do more to celebrate your students than you realize too. I implore you to take the time to celebrate yourself and how you show up for your student writers. We give so much to our students and our profession. We deserve to celebrate ourselves as we celebrate our student writers.

Writer's Affirmations

I am in love with life itself, and I know my stories are worth telling. I honor myself and my lived experiences when I show up to the blank page. The more I write, the more I love living the life of a writer. Writing helps me know myself and appreciate others. I deserve to celebrate myself!

CONCLUSION

At the beginning of this book, I told you about myself as a reader and how I read *The Hobbit* in class in fifth grade. I also shared how that was when I started to feel like a reader *and* a writer because my teacher, Ms. Corn, wrote back and forth to me in my journal. She made me feel like I had something important to say. She made me feel like my stories mattered.

I invited you on a journey, and now that you're here with me now, at the end of this book, it's clear you were up for the adventure. I hope you enjoyed exploring the six practices that student writers have, know, and do. I find joy in learning new things and I'm sure you do too. In living the life of a writer all these years, I've been given the most beautiful gift. I've discovered that there is more to writing than getting an A+ on an essay in school. Being a writer has shown me how to reconnect with who I am, what really matters to me, and what I am capable of.

Writing has brought me to myself and what I truly care about. I hope this book not only offers this to you but to your students as well. Thinking back to my eleven-year-old self, she didn't realize the epic quest she was embarking on, but I can tell you that the treasure is worth it. To know that you are reading these words and that you've been on your own journey, to know that you are guiding your students and setting them off on their own journey brings me so much joy.

Stepping out of our comfort zones to be the writers in residence for our student writers requires us to live our writing lives out loud and in front of them, no less. Living the life of a writer has its good, bad, and ugly sides. Being vulnerable to share our stories and to share our process is critical for every practice we've explored in this book. Embracing living the life of a writer means showing up for yourself so that you can show up for your students. I've asked you to live the life of a writer *with* your student writers. Although Gandalf isn't with Bilbo every step of the way (just like you won't be there for every single word your student writers put on the page), he instills his belief in Bilbo in a way that allows him to then assume confidence in himself. Your courage and dedication to empowering students as writers has an impact on their lives because you're helping them know how to experience living the life of a writer for themselves. You're helping student writers develop their writing identity, and they will carry that with them their whole lives.

Every good ending requires a bit of retrospection as well as a sense of hope and acknowledgement that more adventures are to come. Here, we'll revisit the six practices we've explored, honor our determination and commitment to student writers, and look to what's next.

AT THE TOP OF THE MOUNTAIN

We've reached the top of the mountain. Up ahead, there's a candle burning in a window that is beckoning us home. But before we head down the mountain, we turn to look over our shoulders and appreciate the view, to appreciate what we've gone through and where we've come from.

There will be more mountains to climb, more obstacles to traverse, more views to appreciate, more to look forward to. But, as I shared in Chapter 6, celebration is integral to living the life of a writer. Let's celebrate all we have explored. Each chapter of this book highlighted one of the six practices writers have, know, and do.

Writers Have a Way to Collect: This chapter was an invitation to living the life of a writer as we explored how student writers might collect ideas. I shared opportunities to collect and an invitation to explore what collecting can look like for you and your student writers.

Writers Have a Writer's Mindset: Shifting our attention to a writer's mindset, we observed and noticed the world around us. We also brought our awareness to our writing identity and ways we can affirm our writing identity. It was in this chapter that we stepped into a writer's mindset.

Writers Know that Writing is a Process: We turned to looking closely and objectively at the writing process. We explored how to expand beyond the traditional stages of the writing process that are typically shared in school and instead, to look at writing as *a* process. We also delved into how each writer and each project might require a different process and how we might support that.

Writers Know Strategies to Help Them Write: We celebrated the power of strategies to support writers through their process. We designed our own free writing habit loop to affirm our writing identities. We also found ways to find strategies to help us based on our needs.

Writers Explore: We acknowledged that writers will need to explore what they need while on the journey of living the life of a writer. We connected back to writer's mindset and how writers explore ideas, their process, and strategies to support them. We embraced a mindset of *what if* to expand our thinking.

Writers Celebrate: And all along, we celebrated! We explored celebration as an ongoing practice. And, maybe most importantly, we looked at how celebration can help writers find joy in living the life of a writer—in school and beyond.

Look at all we have traversed together! There are endless ways for student writers to live these practices. We don't have to know every path, every rock, every shortcut. I hope you feel empowered in having the six practices to call on as you guide student writers. I have learned so much about writing by doing it myself and writing alongside students. When I run into an obstacle, I explore opportunities to work through it or around it. Approaching writing instruction in this way gives student writers ownership and control of their experience. They make their own choices. We're the guide who believes in them from the beginning and nudges them toward their own explorations, discoveries, and revelations.

I'm glad to be on this journey with you and appreciate your efforts to center student writers in your writing instruction. Before we head down the mountain, let me pause and acknowledge you and your efforts. You are not nowhere. You are now here, and that is somewhere. Thank you for being here. Thank you for living the life of a writer and encouraging your students to explore the 6 practices I have shared in this book. I see you, and I celebrate you.

READY, SET, WRITE!

In 2024, I received the Don H. Graves Award for Excellence in the Teaching of Writing from the National Council of Teachers of English. I was proud of myself and shared the news with my family and friends, but when a dear friend wanted to celebrate big with me and offered to organize a dinner with friends, I hesitated.

I've struggled my whole life with being seen. It's part of why I take so much care to center and see the writers I work with. Writing has helped me love myself, honor myself, and cherish myself. If I hadn't had such a powerful experience with writing personally, I'm not sure I'd feel as passionate about helping students explore what it means to live the life of a writer for themselves.

Even as an adult, that self doubt can still creep in. A part of me wanted to shrug off my friend's offer to celebrate me, so I explored that feeling in my notebook. Writing about it helped me see that I was deserving of the celebration and that it was okay to receive the love and enjoy it.

This final chapter would not feel genuine if I wasn't vulnerable in sharing how writing has helped me shift my inner thinking from self doubt to self confidence. Through a consistent writing practice, I've been able to acknowledge my inner critic and work with it but not let it dictate how I live my life. I've worked so hard to see all I have accomplished and how far I have come in a society that is constantly pushing toward productivity. Writing helped me unravel the limiting beliefs I had so I could write my own story...and in turn, write this book.

I am enough.

That is a sentence I had to figure out how to write. A sentence I had to figure out how to write and believe. A sentence I had to figure out how to write and believe and trust.

I'm proud to say that writing has helped me be me, finding joy in making progress at my own pace, spending time exploring what it looks like to balance effort and rest, and feeling free to do what feels fun and expansive and aligned with my values and beliefs.

I wrote this book to show you what practices to consider when it comes to living the life of a writer and how to share these six practices with young people. All along, my goal was to honor you by allowing you to explore opportunities and to take ownership of living the life of a writer for yourself so you can guide student writers. I hope you feel empowered and inspired to center student writers and explore the six practices student writers have, know, and do in your classroom.

Beyond that, I hope you know that you are enough. Just as you are.

The version of you who is reading these words right now deserves to be celebrated. Thank you for being on this journey with me. I'm proud to write alongside you. I'm glad you've chosen to explore what it means to live the life of a writer—for yourself and for your student writers.

Writer's Affirmations

I'm the kind of person who writes to make sense of the world. I write to process and remember and understand what I'm experiencing and what I can learn from it. I live the life of a writer for myself while inspiring others to do the same. I know that when I show up for myself, I'm better able to show up for those I care about. I'm proud to be a writer and to continue to explore what it means to live the life of a writer.

ACKNOWLEDGEMENTS

This book is a celebration of what I've learned so far about living the life of a writer, and I owe an enormous amount of gratitude to the people who have supported me as a writer along the way—my fifth-grade teacher, Ms. Corn, who I mention at the beginning of this book, showed me that my writing mattered; my high school English teachers, Ms. Bacigalupi (now Mrs. Zimmerman), Ms. Urkovich, and Mrs. Clark who showed me the power of a writer's work-shop and treated me like a real writer. I could write about my love of my family and my disdain for Calculus, and they gave me sincere feedback while pushing me to reflect on and develop my craft.

As an adult, connecting with other educators through social media inspired me to start my blog Teach Mentor Texts where I shared texts and how to use them as mentor texts with students. I'm so grateful to Jeff Anderson and his work with mentor texts which showed me the power of sharing snippets of texts with students. I'm equally indebted to Donalyn Miller for sharing how important it is to do what real readers do as she helped me think about what real writers do. Donalyn also sparked my interest in NaNoWriMo, which brought me back to writing for myself.

Being a teacher who writes has given me opportunities to connect with so many amazing writers. From blogging, co-hosting Teachers Write, going to and hosting Edcamp Chicago, being part of Nerdy Book Club and Nerdcamp MI, writing for Choice Literacy, volunteering at 826CHI, presenting at the National Council of Teachers of English Annual Convention, being mentored in Pitch Wars (and then being a mentor), taking Story Studio's Essay Collection in a Year with Megan Stielstra, and presenting at the Illinois Association for Teachers of English—I've met too many amazing humans to name, but you've been part of my journey, and I love you all.

It was at NCTE that I connected with my editor, Terry Thompson, and I'm thankful to him for being cool and calm while also fiercely joyful and supportive. It's been a great experi-ence to work with you and the Stenhouse team.

I'm lucky to have amazing friends who not only see me but make sure I shine. To Alison, Kathy G., Cheryl, Joy, Marcie, Jess, Lisa, Lilian, Lolly, Aliza, Carrie B., Carrie S.-T., Kristine, Adam, Liz, Tillie, Mandy, Bitsy, Kathy F., Dana, Justine, Luz, and The Chellas—thank you from the bottom of my heart for cheering me on.

And finally, a giant thank you to my family. Living the life of a writer takes a lot of time and commitment, and I could not have written this book without their love, support, and encouragement. To my grandparents, Gramma, Grandpa, and Mamita, who taught me in their own unique ways and whose memories I cherish. To my parents, Jack and Silvia, who always knew writing would be in my future. To my aunt, Jane, who always fostered my creativity. To my sister, Jacquie, who always reminds me to keep it fun. To my husband, Chad, who is always there when I need him and always up for an adventure. And to my sons, Jordan and Danny, who have always believed this was possible because they know how to dream big *and* go after their dreams—being your mom is the biggest gift. Thank you for keeping me grounded while also inspiring me to soar.

REFERENCES

Anderson, Jeff. 2005. *Mechanically Inclined: Building Grammar, Usage, and Style Into Writer's Workshop*. Portland, ME: Stenhouse Publishers.

Barry, Lynda. 2014. *Syllabus: Notes from an Accidental Professor*. Montreal: Drawn & Quarterly Publications.

Barry, Lynda. 2024. *What It Is*. Montreal: Drawn & Quarterly Publications.

Berger, Warren. 2014. *A More Beautiful Question: The Power of Inquiry to Spark Breakthrough Ideas*. New York: Bloomsbury USA.

Browne, Mahogany L., Elizabeth Acevedo, and Olivia Gatwood. 2020. *Woke: A Young Poet's Call to Justice*. New York: Roaring Brook Press.

Cardenas, Amanda. 2024. "Four Review Games & Activities for the AP Lang Exam." Mud and Ink Teaching, April 9. www.mudandinkteaching.org/news/aplangexamreview.

Duhigg, Charles. 2012. *The Power of Habit: Why We Do What We Do in Life and Business*. New York: Random House Publishing Group.

Fletcher, Ralph. [2003] 2023. *A Writer's Notebook: Unlocking the Writer Within You*. New York: HarperCollins.

Fletcher, Ralph. 2015. "Ralph Fletcher on Mentor Texts." Interview by Franki Sibberson, Choice Literacy Podcast. May 29. Audio. https://choiceliteracy.com/article/ralph-fletcher-on-mentor-texts-podcast/.

FoxMind. n.d. "Disruptus." FoxMind, Board Game. https://foxmind.com/games/disruptus/.

Gladwell, Malcolm. 2008. *Outliers: The Story of Success*. New York: Little, Brown and Company.

Goldberg, Natalie. 2010. *Writing Down the Bones: Freeing the Writer Within*. Boston, MA: Shambhala.

Hall, Don, and Chris Williams, dirs. 2014. *Big Hero 6*. Disney.

Heard, Georgia. 2016. *Heart Maps: Helping Students Create and Craft Authentic Writing*. Portsmouth, NH: Heinemann.

Joyce, James. [1916] 2024. *A Portrait of the Artist as a Young Man*. New York: Union Square & Co.

Kaye, Phil. 2018. "Before the Internet." Button Poetry. https://buttonpoetry.com/phil-kaye-the-big-tree/.

King, Stephen. 2020. *On Writing: A memoir of the craft*. New York: Scribner.

Miller, Donalyn. 2009. *The Book Whisperer: Awakening the Inner Reader in Every Child*. San Francisco, CA: Jossey-Bass.

Montgomery, Sy. 2018. *How to be a Good Creature: A Memoir in Thirteen Animals*. Boston, MA: Houghton Mifflin Harcourt.

Olivarez, José. 2018. "Rumpus Original Poetry: Three Poems by José Olivarez." The Rumpus, July 5. https://therumpus.net/2018/07/05/rumpus-original-poetry-three-poems-by-jose-olivarez/.

Quintero, Isabel. 2019. *My Papi Has a Motorcycle*. Illustrated by Zeke Peña. New York: Penguin Young Readers Group.

Quote Research. 2024. "Quote Origin: Writing Is Easy; You Just Open a Vein and Bleed." Quote Investigator. https://quoteinvestigator.com/2011/09/14/writing-bleed/.

Ray, Katie W. 2010. *In Pictures and in Words: Teaching the Qualities of Good Writing Through Illustration Study*. Portsmouth, NH: Heinemann.

Serravallo, Jennifer. 2017. *The Writing Strategies Book: Your Everything Guide to Developing Skilled Writers*. Portsmouth, NH: Heinemann.

Snyder, Blake. 2005. *Save the Cat! The Last Book on Screenwriting You'll Ever Need*. Studio City, CA: Michael Wiese Productions.

Swift, Jonathan. [1726] 2022. *Gulliver's Travels*. Cambridge, England: Cambridge University Press.

Tolkien, John Ronald R. 2012. *The Hobbit, Or, There and Back Again*. Boston, MA: Houghton Mifflin Harcourt.

Vincent, Jen, and Carrie Baughcum. 2025. Sketchnoting. Personal Interview. January 6.

Vincent, Jen. 2025. "Habit Loops – Exploring a Writer's Mindset." YouTube, February 16. www.youtube.com/watch?v=cmHBT5-Vrlo.

Wilkins, Kara. 2013. "Grudgeball. A Review Game Where Kids Attack!" To Engage Them All, February 20. http://toengagethemall.blogspot.com/2013/02/grudgeball-review-game-where-kids-attack.html.

Woodson, Jacqueline. 2018. *The Day You Begin*. New York: Penguin Young Readers Group.

INDEX

For Product Safety Concerns and Information,
please contact our EU representative GPSR@taylorandfrancis.com
Taylor & Francis Verlag GmbH, Kaufingerstraße 24,
80331 München, Germany

Printed by Integrated Books International,
United States of America